The Cookie Book

Publications International, Ltd.

Some of the products listed in this publication may be in limited distribution.

Pictured on the front cover: Frosted Butter Cookies *(page 166)*.
Pictured on the back jacket flap: Autumn Pumpkin Bars *(page 222)*.
Pictured on the back cover *(top to bottom):* Extra-Chocolatey Brownie Cookies *(page 56)*, Tea Cookies *(page 76)* and Black & White Sandwich Cookies *(page 78)*.

ISBN: 978-1-68022-151-0

Library of Congress Control Number: 2015934780

Manufactured in China.

8 7 6 5 4 3 2 1

Microwave Cooking: Microwave ovens vary in wattage. Use the cooking times as guidelines and check for doneness before adding more time.

Acknowledgments

The publisher would like to thank the companies and organizations listed below for the use of their recipes and photographs in this publication.

ACH Food Companies, Inc.

The Hershey Company

Contents

The Perfect Present

Homemade cookies always make wonderful gifts. Of course they're standard at the holidays, but they also make great gifts any time of the year: Mother's Day, Father's Day, Valentine's Day, birthdays, housewarming gifts, thank-you gifts and party favors.

MAKING ENOUGH

Before you shop for ingredients, plan how many cookie gifts you will need and how many cookies will be included in each gift. Decide how many cookies each gift will contain (for example, 12 for an individual, 24 for a family and 40 for a workplace) and calculate how many cookies you will need. If you need more cookies than a single recipe yields, make separate batches of dough instead of doubling the recipe.

If you're planning on giving elaborately decorated cookies like Frosted Butter Cookies (page 166), consider also including one or two simple high-yield cookies like White-Chocolate-Macadamia Nut Cookies (page 18), Gooey Thumbprints (page 60) or Chocolate-Dipped Cinnamon Thins (page 178). You'll still have a fabulously impressive cookie gift but in a fraction of the time.

When you're making a lot of cookies, plan on one day for making dough and one day for baking (and maybe even another day for decorating). Most cookie dough can be made ahead and refrigerated for a day or two; in fact, some dough requires it and in many cases this improves the flavor of the finished cookie. Wrap the dough tightly in plastic wrap, and label it if you're making more than one type.

DECORATING

Many cookies can be made extra special with a few simple decorating techniques.

• **Cookie glaze.** Sift 1 cup of powdered sugar into a small bowl. Stir in milk, cream or citrus juice by teaspoonfuls until the glaze reaches drizzling consistency. Drizzle the glaze over your cookies with a small spoon or fork and then sprinkle with decorating sugars. Let the cookies stand until the glaze is set.

• **Chocolate dipped.** Melt high-quality bittersweet chocolate (60 percent cacao) in a small saucepan over low heat until melted, stirring constantly. Transfer the chocolate to a small deep bowl. Dip each cookie halfway into the chocolate, scraping the bottoms on the edge of the bowl to remove excess chocolate, then place the cookies on a waxed paper-lined baking sheet. Sprinkle with multicolored sprinkles or decors and let the cookies stand at room temperature or refrigerate until the chocolate is set. Try this with Triple Chipper Monsters (page 12), Refrigerator Cookies (page 34), Black and White Sandwich Cookies (page 78) or Chocolate Strawberry Stackers (page 84).

PACKAGING

When you're giving several different kinds of cookies, be aware that cookies packaged together will affect each other's flavors; subtly flavored cookies like butter cookies or shortbread will pick up stronger flavors like coffee, chocolate or gingerbread. If you're planning on packing all the cookies in one box or basket, wrap the cookies with the strong flavor separately in a cellophane bag before boxing them.

TYPES OF PACKAGES

Keep an eye out all year for interesting packaging and, if you have storage space, stock up on containers during post-holiday sales. Craft supply stores and online retailers are excellent resources for cookie packaging.

• **Tins and boxes.** These work well for fragile cookies, or cookies that will be shipped. Look for bakery boxes at craft supply stores or online, or reuse solid decorative gift boxes. Pack cookies in cellophane bags or line the container with tissue paper, decorative dish towel or cloth napkin before loosely packing with cookies.

• **Cellophane bags.** Clear bags are available in various shapes and sizes, ranging from small enough for individual cookies to large enough to hold an entire batch of cookies. Close the bags with the included twist-ties and then secure with ribbon. Add a decorative label, or place in a gift bag.

• **Vintage china plates or bowls, glass cake plates, cookie jars or brightly colored baking dishes.** Vintage shops, flea markets and garage sales are great sources for quirky and unique containers for cookies. Arrange cookies on the dish or platter, then tightly wrap with clear clingy plastic wrap or cellophane and tie with a bow.

• **Trays.** Party supply stores sell a variety of disposable and reusable trays in colors, patterns and metallic finishes. Trays are perfect for large cookie displays at parties or offices.

GIFT IDEAS

• **Study Gift for the Student.** Package Holiday Biscotti (page 168) or Apricot Biscotti (page 70) in wide-mouth half-gallon canning jars, glass canister jars or cellophane bags and include coffee, tea or hot chocolate mix.

• **Ultimate Holiday Cookie Tray.** Holiday Triple Chocolate Yule Logs (page 194), Chocolate Thumbprint Cookies (page 68), Gingerbread People (page 192), Chocolate Cherry Cookies (page 74), Browned Butter Spritz Cookies (page 180) and Rum Fruitcake Cookies (page 174). Arrange the cookies on a vintage holiday tray, on a disposable plastic tray or in a large hat box.

• **Housewarming Gift.** Make bar cookies in a new 13x9-inch baking pan (see pages 102–127). Cool completely and cut into squares, then wrap the whole pan with cellophane and tie with a bow. Or make the Chocolate Chip Skillet Cookie (page 24) in a new cast iron skillet and tie an oven mitt and a spatula to the handle with ribbon.

• **Wedding or Baby Shower Party Favors.** Wrap single cookies or pairs of cookies in small cellophane bags and tie with color-coordinated ribbon. Try Wedding Bells (page 206), Yummy Rattles (208) or Letters of the Alphabet (page 230) in the happy couple's or baby's initials.

Classics for Christmas

Peanut Blossoms

¼ cup sugar

1 package (about 15 ounces) yellow cake mix

1 cup peanut butter

⅓ cup butter, softened

1 egg

50 milk chocolate kiss candies, unwrapped

1. Preheat oven to 350°F. Line cookie sheets with parchment paper. Place sugar in small bowl.

2. Beat cake mix, peanut butter, butter and egg in large bowl with electric mixer at medium speed until well blended.

3. Shape dough into 1-inch balls; roll in sugar. Place 2 inches apart on prepared cookie sheets. Press one candy into center of each ball, flattening dough slightly.

4. Bake 10 minutes or until lightly browned. Cool on cookie sheets 2 minutes. Remove to wire racks; cool completely.

Makes about 4 dozen cookies

Basic Oatmeal Cookies

2 cups old-fashioned oats
1⅓ cups all-purpose flour
¾ teaspoon baking soda
½ teaspoon baking powder
½ teaspoon salt
1 cup packed brown sugar

¾ cup (1½ sticks) butter, softened
¼ cup granulated sugar
1 egg
1 tablespoon honey
1 teaspoon vanilla

1. Preheat oven to 350°F. Line cookie sheets with parchment paper.

2. Combine oats, flour, baking soda, baking powder and salt in medium bowl.

3. Beat brown sugar, butter and granulated sugar in large bowl with electric mixer at medium speed until light and fluffy. Add egg, honey and vanilla; beat until well blended. Gradually add flour mixture about ½ cup at a time; beat at low speed just until blended. Drop dough by tablespoonfuls about 2 inches apart onto prepared cookie sheets.

4. Bake 11 to 15 minutes or until cookies are puffed and golden. *Do not overbake.* Cool on cookie sheets 5 minutes. Remove to wire racks; cool completely.

Makes 3 dozen cookies

BUTTERSCOTCH-COCONUT OATMEAL COOKIES: Prepare Basic Oatmeal Cookies with the following variations. Decrease oats to ¾ cup and brown sugar to ½ cup. Melt ½ cup butterscotch chips and add to sugar mixture with egg. Stir ½ cup flaked coconut and ½ cup chopped pecans into dough with flour mixture.

Triple Chipper Monsters

2½ cups all-purpose flour
1 teaspoon baking soda
¾ teaspoon salt
1 cup (2 sticks) butter, softened
1 cup packed brown sugar
½ cup granulated sugar

2 eggs
2 teaspoons vanilla
2 cups semisweet chocolate chips
½ cup white chocolate chips
½ cup butterscotch or peanut butter chips

1. Preheat oven to 350°F.

2. Combine flour, baking soda and salt in medium bowl.

3. Beat butter, brown sugar and granulated sugar in large bowl of electric mixer at medium speed until light and fluffy. Beat in eggs and vanilla until blended. Gradually beat in flour mixture at low speed until well blended. Stir in chips. Drop dough by scant ¼ cupfuls 3 inches apart onto ungreased cookie sheets. Lightly flatten dough with fingertips.

4. Bake 12 to 14 minutes or until edges are set and golden brown. Cool cookies on cookie sheets 2 minutes. Remove to wire racks; cool completely.

Makes about 22 cookies

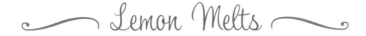

Lemon Melts

2 cups all-purpose flour
½ teaspoon cream of tartar
½ teaspoon baking soda
½ cup powdered sugar
½ cup packed brown sugar

½ cup canola oil
½ cup (1 stick) butter, melted
1 tablespoon lemon juice
1 tablespoon vanilla
1½ teaspoons almond extract

1. Preheat oven to 350°F. Line cookie sheets with parchment paper.

2. Combine flour, cream of tartar and baking soda in medium bowl.

3. Beat powdered sugar, brown sugar, oil, butter, lemon juice, vanilla and almond extract in large bowl with electric mixer at medium speed until smooth. Gradually beat in flour mixture until stiff dough forms. Drop dough by rounded tablespoonfuls 2 inches apart onto prepared cookie sheets; flatten slightly with fork.

4. Bake 20 minutes or until edges are lightly browned. Cool on cookie sheets 1 minute. Remove to wire racks; cool completely.

Makes about 3½ dozen cookies

Snickerdoodles

¾ cup plus 1 tablespoon sugar, divided

2 teaspoons ground cinnamon, divided

1⅓ cups all-purpose flour

1 teaspoon cream of tartar

½ teaspoon baking soda

½ cup (1 stick) butter, softened

1 egg

1 cup cinnamon baking chips

1 cup raisins (optional)

1. Preheat oven to 400°F. Combine 1 tablespoon sugar and 1 teaspoon cinnamon in small bowl.

2. Combine flour, remaining 1 teaspoon cinnamon, cream of tartar and baking soda in medium bowl.

3. Beat remaining ¾ cup sugar and butter in large bowl with electric mixer at medium speed until creamy. Beat in egg. Gradually add flour mixture to sugar mixture, beating at low speed until stiff dough forms. Stir in cinnamon chips and raisins, if desired. Roll dough into 1-inch balls; roll in cinnamon-sugar mixture. Place on ungreased cookie sheets.

4. Bake 10 minutes or until set. *Do not overbake.* Remove to wire racks; cool completely.

Makes about 3 dozen cookies

White Chocolate Macadamia Nut Cookies

1½ cups all-purpose flour

½ teaspoon salt

¼ teaspoon baking soda

1½ cups packed brown sugar

⅔ cup shortening

2 eggs

1 teaspoon vanilla

1 cup white chocolate chips

1 cup macadamia nuts, coarsely chopped

1. Preheat oven to 375°F.

2. Combine flour, salt and baking soda in medium bowl.

3. Beat brown sugar and shortening in large bowl with electric mixer at medium-high speed until light and fluffy. Add eggs, one at a time, beating well after each addition. Beat in vanilla. Add flour mixture; beat at low speed just until blended. Stir in white chocolate chips and nuts. Drop dough by rounded tablespoonfuls 2 inches apart onto ungreased cookie sheets.

4. Bake 9 to 11 minutes or until cookies are set. Cool on cookie sheet 2 minutes. Remove to wire racks; cool completely.

Makes about 3 dozen cookies

Classic
Chocolate Chip Cookies

1¼ **cups all-purpose flour**
½ **teaspoon salt**
½ **teaspoon baking soda**
½ **cup (1 stick) butter, softened**
½ **cup granulated sugar**
¼ **cup packed brown sugar**

1 **egg**
1 **teaspoon vanilla**
1 **cup semisweet chocolate chips**
½ **cup coarsely chopped walnuts (optional)**

1. Preheat oven to 350°F. Line cookie sheets with parchment paper.

2. Combine flour, salt and baking soda in medium bowl.

3. Beat butter, granulated sugar and brown sugar in large bowl with electric mixer at medium speed until light and fluffy. Add egg and vanilla; beat until well blended. Add flour mixture; beat just until blended. Stir in chocolate chips and walnuts, if desired. Drop tablespoonfuls of dough 2 inches apart onto prepared cookie sheets.

4. Bake 10 to 12 minutes or until edges are lightly browned. Cool on cookie sheets 1 minute. Remove to wire racks; cool completely.

Makes about 3 dozen cookies

Butter Pecan Crisps

2½ cups sifted all-purpose flour

1 teaspoon baking soda

1 cup (2 sticks) butter, softened

¾ cup granulated sugar

¾ cup packed brown sugar

½ teaspoon salt

2 eggs

1 teaspoon vanilla

1½ cups finely ground pecans

30 pecan halves

4 ounces semisweet chocolate

1 tablespoon shortening

1. Preheat oven to 375°F. Line cookie sheets with parchment paper.

2. Combine flour and baking soda in small bowl.

3. Beat butter, granulated sugar, brown sugar and salt in large bowl with electric mixer at medium speed until light and fluffy. Add eggs, one at a time, beating well after each addition. Beat in vanilla and ground pecans. Gradually stir in flour mixture.

4. Spoon dough into large pastry bag fitted with ⅜-inch round tip; fill bag halfway. Shake down dough to remove air bubbles. Hold bag perpendicular to, and about ½ inch above, prepared cookie sheets. Pipe dough into 1¼-inch balls, spacing 3 inches apart. Cut each pecan half lengthwise into 2 slivers. Press 1 sliver in center of each dough ball.

5. Bake 10 minutes or until lightly browned. Cool on cookie sheets 5 minutes. Remove to wire racks; cool completely.

6. Melt chocolate and shortening in small heavy saucepan over low heat, stirring constantly until melted and smooth. Drizzle over cookies. Let stand until set.

Makes about 5 dozen cookies

Chocolate Chip Skillet Cookie

1³/₄ cups all-purpose flour

1 teaspoon baking soda

1 teaspoon salt

³/₄ cup (1¹/₂ sticks) butter, softened

³/₄ cup packed brown sugar

¹/₂ cup granulated sugar

2 eggs

1 teaspoon vanilla

1 package (12 ounces) semisweet chocolate chips

Sea salt (optional)

Ice cream (optional)

1. Preheat oven to 350°F.

2. Combine flour, baking soda and 1 teaspoon salt in medium bowl.

3. Beat butter, brown sugar and granulated sugar in large bowl with electric mixer at medium speed until creamy. Beat in eggs and vanilla until well blended. Gradually beat in flour at low speed just until blended. Stir in chocolate chips. Press batter evenly into well-seasoned large (10-inch) cast iron skillet. Sprinkle lightly with sea salt, if desired.

4. Bake about 35 minutes or until top and edges are golden brown but cookie is still soft in center. Cool on wire rack 10 minutes before cutting into wedges. Serve warm with ice cream, if desired.

Makes 8 servings

Cashew-Lemon Shortbread Cookies

½ cup roasted cashew nuts

1 cup (2 sticks) butter, softened

½ cup plus 2 tablespoons sugar, divided

2 teaspoons lemon extract

1 teaspoon vanilla

2½ cups all-purpose flour

1. Preheat oven to 325°F.

2. Place cashews in food processor; process until finely ground. Add butter, ½ cup sugar, lemon extract and vanilla; process until well blended. Add flour; pulse until dough begins to form a ball.

3. Shape dough into 1½-inch balls; roll in remaining 2 tablespoons sugar. Place 2 inches apart on ungreased cookie sheets; flatten slightly.

4. Bake 17 to 19 minutes or just until set. Remove to wire racks; cool completely.

Makes about 2½ dozen cookies

New England Raisin Spice Cookies

2¼ cups all-purpose flour
2 teaspoons baking soda
1 teaspoon salt
¾ teaspoon ground cinnamon
¼ teaspoon ground ginger
¼ teaspoon ground cloves
⅛ teaspoon ground allspice

1½ cups raisins
1 cup packed brown sugar
½ cup shortening
¼ cup (½ stick) butter
1 egg
⅓ cup molasses
Granulated sugar

1. Combine flour, baking soda, salt, cinnamon, ginger, cloves and allspice in medium bowl. Stir in raisins.

2. Beat brown sugar, shortening and butter in large bowl with electric mixer at medium speed until creamy. Add egg and molasses; beat until fluffy. Gradually add flour mixture, stirring until just blended. Cover; refrigerate at least 2 hours.

3. Preheat oven to 350°F. Shape heaping tablespoons of dough into balls. Roll in granulated sugar. Place 2 inches apart on ungreased cookie sheets.

4. Bake 8 minutes or until golden brown. Cool on cookie sheets 1 minute. Remove to wire racks; cool completely. Store in airtight container.

Makes about 5 dozen cookies

Flourless Peanut Butter Cookies

1 cup packed brown sugar
1 cup creamy peanut butter
1 egg, lightly beaten

$1/2$ cup semisweet chocolate chips, melted

1. Preheat oven to 350°F. Beat brown sugar, peanut butter and egg in medium bowl until blended and smooth.

2. Shape dough into 24 ($1\frac{1}{2}$-inch) balls. Place 2 inches apart on ungreased cookie sheets. Flatten dough slightly with fork.

3. Bake 10 to 12 minutes or until set. Remove to wire racks; cool completely. Drizzle with chocolate.

Makes 2 dozen cookies

VARIATION: Press a milk chocolate star or milk chocolate kiss candy into each cookie ball before baking instead of drizzling with melted chocolate.

Black and White Hearts

1 cup (2 sticks) butter,
softened

3/4 cup sugar

3 ounces cream cheese,
softened

1 egg

1 1/2 teaspoons vanilla

3 cups all-purpose flour

1 cup semisweet chocolate
chips

2 tablespoons shortening

1. Beat butter, sugar, cream cheese, egg and vanilla in large bowl with electric mixer at medium speed until light and fluffy. Add flour; beat until well blended. Divide dough in half; wrap each half in plastic wrap. Refrigerate 2 hours or until firm.

2. Preheat oven to 375°F. Roll dough to 1/8-inch thickness on lightly floured surface. Cut dough with lightly floured 2-inch heart-shaped cookie cutter. Place cutouts 1 inch apart on ungreased cookie sheets. Bake 7 to 10 minutes or until edges are lightly browned. Immediately remove to wire racks; cool completely.

3. Melt chocolate chips and shortening in small saucepan over low heat, stirring constantly until smooth. Dip half of each heart into melted chocolate. Refrigerate on cookie sheets or trays lined with waxed paper until chocolate is set. Store covered in refrigerator.

Makes about 3 1/2 dozen cookies

Refrigerator Cookies

1¾ cups all-purpose flour
¼ teaspoon baking soda
¼ teaspoon salt
½ cup granulated sugar
¼ cup light corn syrup
¼ cup (½ stick) butter,
  softened

2 eggs
1 teaspoon vanilla
  Decors, sprinkles and
  colored sugars

1. Combine flour, baking soda and salt in medium bowl.

2. Beat granulated sugar, corn syrup and butter in large bowl with electric mixer at medium speed. Add eggs and vanilla; beat until well blended. Stir in flour mixture at low speed just until blended.

3. Shape dough into two logs 1½ inches in diameter. Wrap in plastic wrap. Freeze 1 hour.

4. Preheat oven to 350°F. Line cookie sheets with parchment paper. Cut dough into ¼-inch-thick slices; place 1 inch apart on prepared cookie sheets. Sprinkle with colored sugar, if desired.

5. Bake 8 to 10 minutes or until edges are golden brown. Remove to wire racks; cool completely.

Makes about 4 dozen cookies

VARIATIONS: For citrus cookies, stir in 1 teaspoon grated orange peel into butter mixture. For chocolate chip cookies, stir ½ cup mini chocolate chips into dough with flour mixture. For chocolate cookies, stir 2 tablespoons unsweetened cocoa powder into flour mixture. For sugar-rimmed cookies, roll logs in colored sugar before slicing.

Chocolate Decadence

Classic Brownies

1 cup all-purpose flour

½ cup unsweetened cocoa
   powder

½ teaspoon salt

½ teaspoon baking powder

½ cup (1 stick) butter, softened

2 ounces cream cheese

1 cup sugar

2 eggs

1 teaspoon vanilla

½ cup semisweet chocolate
   chips (optional)

1. Preheat oven to 350°F. Spray 9-inch square baking pan with nonstick cooking spray. Combine flour, cocoa, salt and baking powder in small bowl.

2. Beat butter and cream cheese in large bowl with electric mixer at high speed until smooth. Add sugar, eggs and vanilla; beat until smooth. Add flour mixture; mix at low speed just until blended. Spread batter in prepared pan.

3. Bake 15 to 20 minutes or until toothpick inserted into center comes out clean. Sprinkle with chocolate chips, if desired; cool completely in pan. Cut into squares or rectangles.

Makes 2 dozen brownies

Chocolate Marshmallow Drops

1¾ cups all-purpose flour

⅓ cup unsweetened cocoa powder

1 teaspoon baking soda

½ teaspoon salt

1 cup sugar

½ cup (1 stick) butter

¼ cup milk

1 egg

1 teaspoon vanilla

16 to 18 large marshmallows, cut into halves

Chocolate Glaze (recipe follows)

36 pecan halves (optional)

1. Preheat oven to 350°F. Combine flour, cocoa, baking soda and salt in small bowl.

2. Beat sugar and butter in large bowl with electric mixer at medium speed until light and fluffy. Add milk, egg and vanilla; beat until well blended. Gradually add flour mixture, beating until blended. Drop dough by rounded teaspoonfuls onto ungreased cookie sheets.

3. Bake 8 minutes. Remove from oven; gently press 1 marshmallow half, cut side down, onto each cookie. Return to oven 3 to 4 minutes or until marshmallows are softened and cookies are set. Cool on cookie sheets 1 minute. Remove to wire racks; cool completely.

4. Prepare Chocolate Glaze; drizzle over cookies. Top with pecans, if desired.

Makes about 3 dozen cookies

CHOCOLATE GLAZE: Combine ⅓ cup whipping cream and 1 tablespoon butter in small saucepan; bring to a boil over high heat. Place ½ cup semisweet chocolate chips in medium bowl. Pour cream mixture over chocolate; let stand 5 minutes. Stir until smooth.

Malted Milk Cookies

1 cup (2 sticks) butter, softened
¾ cup granulated sugar
¾ cup packed brown sugar
1 teaspoon baking soda
2 eggs
2 ounces unsweetened chocolate, melted and cooled to room temperature

1 teaspoon vanilla
2¼ cups all-purpose flour
½ cup malted milk powder
1 cup chopped malted milk balls

1. Preheat oven to 375°F.

2. Beat butter in large bowl with electric mixer at medium speed until creamy. Add granulated sugar, brown sugar and baking soda; beat until blended. Add eggs, chocolate and vanilla; beat until well blended. Beat in flour and malted milk powder until blended. Stir in malted milk balls. Drop dough by rounded tablespoonfuls 2 inches apart onto ungreased cookie sheets.

3. Bake about 10 minutes or until edges are set. Cool on cookie sheets 1 minute. Remove to wire racks; cool completely.

Makes about 4 dozen cookies

Mocha Brownie Cookies

2½ cups all-purpose flour

⅓ cup unsweetened cocoa powder

1 teaspoon baking soda

1 teaspoon baking powder

1 teaspoon salt

1 cup granulated sugar

¾ cup packed brown sugar

½ cup (1 stick) butter, softened

¼ cup sour cream

1 tablespoon instant coffee, dissolved in 2 tablespoons hot water

2 eggs

1½ cups semisweet chocolate chips

1. Preheat oven to 325°F. Combine flour, cocoa, baking soda, baking powder and salt in medium bowl.

2. Beat granulated sugar, brown sugar, butter, sour cream and coffee mixture in large bowl with electric mixer at medium speed until creamy. Add eggs, one at a time, beating well after each addition until batter is light and fluffy.

3. Gradually add flour mixture to butter mixture, beating at low speed until just blended. Beat at medium speed 1 minute or until well blended. Stir in chocolate chips. Drop dough by rounded tablespoonfuls onto ungreased cookie sheets.

4. Bake 9 to 11 minutes or until slight imprint remains when pressed with finger. Cool on cookie sheets 3 minutes. Remove to wire racks; cool completely.

Makes 5 to 6 dozen cookies

Dark Chocolate Dreams

½ cup all-purpose flour
¾ teaspoon ground cinnamon
½ teaspoon baking powder
¼ teaspoon salt
16 ounces bittersweet chocolate, coarsely chopped
¼ cup (½ stick) butter
1½ cups sugar

3 eggs
1 teaspoon vanilla
1 package (12 ounces) white chocolate chips
1 cup chopped pecans, lightly toasted*

*To toast pecans, spread in single layer on ungreased baking sheet. Bake in preheated 350°F oven 5 to 7 minutes or until light brown, stirring occasionally

1. Preheat oven to 350°F. Line cookie sheets with parchment paper. Combine flour, cinnamon, baking powder and salt in small bowl.

2. Combine chocolate and butter in large microwavable bowl. Microwave on HIGH 2 minutes; stir. Microwave 1 to 2 minutes, stirring after 1 minute, or until chocolate is melted. Cool slightly.

3. Beat sugar, eggs and vanilla with electric mixer at medium-high speed about 6 minutes or until very thick and pale. Reduce speed to low; gradually beat in chocolate mixture until well blended. Gradually beat in flour mixture until blended. Fold in white chocolate chips and pecans.

4. Drop dough by level ⅓ cupfuls 3 inches apart onto prepared cookie sheets. Flatten dough into 4-inch circles with fingers covered in plastic wrap.

5. Bake 12 minutes or just until firm and surface begins to crack. *Do not overbake.* Cool cookies on cookie sheets 2 minutes. Remove to wire racks; cool completely.

Makes 10 to 12 cookies

Surprise Cookies

2 ounces semisweet baking chocolate, coarsely chopped

1¼ cups all-purpose flour

½ teaspoon baking powder

¼ teaspoon salt

½ cup (1 stick) butter, softened

½ cup sugar

1 egg

1 teaspoon vanilla

Fillings: drained maraschino cherries or candied cherries; white chocolate chunks; chocolate chunks; raspberry jam or apricot preserves

Sprinkles or nonpareils (optional)

1. Preheat oven to 350°F. Spray 12 mini (1¾-inch) muffin cups with nonstick cooking spray.

2. Melt semisweet chocolate in small heavy saucepan over low heat, stirring constantly; remove from heat. Combine flour, baking powder and salt in small bowl.

3. Beat butter and sugar in large bowl with electric mixer at medium speed 2 minutes or until light and fluffy. Beat in egg and vanilla. Beat in melted chocolate. Gradually add flour mixture, beating at low speed until blended.

4. Drop dough by level teaspoonfuls into prepared muffin cups. Form small indentation in centers; fill with desired fillings. Top with heaping teaspoonful of dough, smoothing top lightly. Top with sprinkles, if desired.

5. Bake 15 to 17 minutes or until set. Cool completely in pan.

Makes 1 dozen cookies

Chocolate-Coconut-Toffee Delights

½ cup all-purpose flour
¼ teaspoon baking powder
¼ teaspoon salt
1 package (12 ounces) semisweet chocolate chips, divided
¼ cup butter (½ stick), cut into small pieces

¾ cup packed brown sugar
2 eggs, beaten
1 teaspoon vanilla
1½ cups flaked coconut
1 cup toffee baking bits
½ cup dark chocolate chips
1 teaspoon shortening

1. Preheat oven to 350°F. Line cookie sheets with parchment paper. Combine flour, baking powder and salt in small bowl.

2. Place 1 cup semisweet chocolate chips and butter in large microwavable bowl. Microwave on HIGH 1 minute; stir. Microwave at additional 30-second intervals, stirring after each interval until mixture is melted and smooth.

3. Beat brown sugar, eggs and vanilla in large bowl with electric mixer at medium speed. Beat in chocolate mixture until well blended. Add flour mixture; beat at low speed until blended. Stir in coconut, toffee bits and remaining 1 cup semisweet chocolate chips. Drop dough by heaping ⅓ cupfuls 3 inches apart onto prepared cookie sheets. Flatten with rubber spatula into 3½-inch circles.

4. Bake 15 to 17 minutes or until edges are firm to the touch. Cool on cookie sheets 2 minutes; slide parchment paper and cookies onto wire racks. Cool completely.

5. For chocolate drizzle, melt dark chocolate chips and shortening in small microwavable bowl on HIGH 1 minutes; stir. Microwave at additional 30-second intervals until smooth. Drizzle over cookies using fork. Let stand until set.

Makes 1 dozen large cookies

Chunky Double Chocolate Cookies

4 ounces unsweetened chocolate, chopped

2 cups all-purpose flour

1½ teaspoons baking powder

½ teaspoon salt

1½ cups packed brown sugar

¾ cup (1½ sticks) butter, softened

1 teaspoon vanilla

2 eggs

12 ounces white chocolate, chopped

1 cup chopped nuts (optional)

1. Preheat oven to 350°F. Melt unsweetened chocolate in small saucepan over low heat, stirring constantly. Cool slightly.

2. Combine flour, baking powder and salt in medium bowl.

3. Beat brown sugar, butter and vanilla in large bowl with electric mixer at medium speed until light and fluffy. Add eggs; beat until well blended. Beat in melted chocolate. Gradually add flour mixture, beating well at low speed after each addition. Stir in white chocolate and nuts, if desired. Drop by rounded tablespoonfuls 2 inches apart onto ungreased cookie sheets.

4. Bake 11 to 12 minutes or until set. Cool on cookie sheets 1 minute. Remove to wire racks; cool completely. Store in airtight container up to 1 week.

Makes about 3 dozen cookies

Deep Dark Chocolate Drops

1¼ cups all-purpose flour

¼ cup unsweetened cocoa powder

½ teaspoon baking soda

½ teaspoon salt

1½ cups semisweet chocolate chips, divided

½ cup (1 stick) butter, softened

½ cup granulated sugar

¼ cup packed brown sugar

1 egg

2 tablespoons milk

1 teaspoon vanilla

1. Preheat oven to 350°F. Line cookie sheets with parchment paper. Combine flour, cocoa, baking soda and salt in medium bowl.

2. Place ½ cup chocolate chips in small microwavable bowl. Microwave on HIGH 1 minute; stir. Microwave at additional 30-second intervals, stirring after each interval, until melted and smooth. Cool slightly.

3. Beat butter, granulated sugar and brown sugar in large bowl with electric mixer at medium speed until light and fluffy. Add egg, milk, vanilla and melted chocolate; beat until well blended. Add flour mixture; beat just until blended. Stir in remaining 1 cup chocolate chips. Drop dough by rounded tablespoonfuls 2 inches apart onto prepared cookie sheets.

4. Bake 10 minutes or until set. Cool on cookie sheets 2 minutes. Remove to wire racks; cool completely.

Makes about 3 dozen cookies

Mocha Dots

1 tablespoon instant coffee granules
2 tablespoons hot water
1¹⁄₂ cups all-purpose flour
¹⁄₄ cup unsweetened cocoa powder
¹⁄₂ teaspoon baking soda
¹⁄₂ teaspoon salt

¹⁄₂ cup (1 stick) butter, softened
¹⁄₂ cup granulated sugar
¹⁄₄ cup packed brown sugar
1 egg
1 teaspoon vanilla
72 chocolate nonpareil candies (about 1 inch in diameter)

1. Preheat oven to 350°F. Line cookie sheets with parchment paper. Dissolve instant coffee granules in hot water; cool slightly. Combine flour, cocoa, baking soda and salt in medium bowl.

2. Beat butter, granulated sugar and brown sugar in large bowl with electric mixer at medium speed until light and fluffy. Add egg, coffee mixture and vanilla; beat until well blended. Add flour mixture; beat until well blended.

3. Shape level teaspoonfuls of dough into balls; place 2 inches apart on prepared cookie sheets. Gently press 1 candy onto center of each ball. (Do not press candies too far into dough balls. Cookies will spread around candies as they bake.)

4. Bake 7 to 8 minutes or until set and no longer shiny. Cool on cookie sheets 2 minutes. Remove to wire racks; cool completely.

Makes 6 dozen cookies

Extra-Chocolatey Brownie Cookies

2 cups all-purpose flour

$\frac{1}{2}$ cup unsweetened Dutch process cocoa powder

1 teaspoon baking soda

$\frac{3}{4}$ teaspoon salt

1 cup (2 sticks) butter, softened

1 cup packed brown sugar

$\frac{1}{2}$ cup granulated sugar

2 eggs

2 teaspoons vanilla

1 package (11 ounces) semisweet chocolate chunks

2 cups coarsely chopped walnuts or pecans

1. Preheat oven to 375°F. Whisk flour, cocoa, baking soda and salt in medium bowl until well blended.

2. Beat butter in large bowl with electric mixer at medium speed 1 minute or until light and fluffy. Add brown sugar and granulated sugar; beat 2 minutes or until fluffy. Add eggs and vanilla; beat until well blended. Add flour mixture; beat at low speed until blended. Stir in chocolate chunks and walnuts.

3. Drop dough by heaping tablespoonfuls 2 inches apart onto ungreased cookie sheets; flatten slightly.

4. Bake 12 minutes or until set. Cool on cookie sheets 2 minutes. Remove to wire racks; cool completely. Store in airtight container at room temperature up to 4 days.

Makes 3 dozen cookies

Festive Fruit Favorites

Golden Apricot Cookies

Easy All-Purpose Cookie Dough (page 60)
12 Mediterranean-style dried apricots or glacé apricots

1 cup apricot jam

1. Prepare Easy All-Purpose Cookie Dough through step 1. Shape dough into 10-inch log. Wrap in plastic wrap; refrigerate 1 hour.

2. Preheat oven to 300°F. Cut log into ½-inch-thick slices; place on ungreased cookie sheets. Bake 20 to 25 minutes or until cookies are set and lightly browned. Cool on cookie sheets 5 minutes. Remove to wire racks; cool completely.

3. Separate apricots into halves. Arrange one half on each cookie. Place jam in small saucepan. Bring to a simmer over medium-low heat; cook 2 minutes or until melted. Strain into small bowl; discard solids. Spoon 1 teaspoon apricot glaze over each apricot to cover. Set aside 1 hour or until glaze sets.

Makes about 2 dozen cookies

Gooey Thumbprints

Easy All-Purpose Cookie Dough (recipe follows)

¼ cup strawberry, grape or apricot jam or chocolate-hazelnut spread

1. Prepare and chill cookie dough as directed. Preheat oven to 300°F.

2. Shape dough into 1-inch balls; place 1 inch apart on ungreased cookie sheets. Make small indentation in each ball with thumb; fill with heaping ¼ teaspoon jam.

3. Bake 25 to 27 minutes or until tops of cookies are light golden brown. Cool on cookie sheets 1 minute. Remove to wire racks; cool completely.

Makes about 3 dozen cookies

Easy All-Purpose Cookie Dough

1 cup (2 sticks) butter, softened
½ cup powdered sugar
2 tablespoons packed brown sugar

¼ teaspoon salt
1 egg
2 cups all-purpose flour

1. Beat butter, powdered sugar, brown sugar and salt in large bowl with electric mixer at medium speed 2 minutes or until light and fluffy. Add egg; beat until well blended. Add flour, ½ cup at a time, beating well at low speed after each addition.

2. Shape dough into disc; wrap tightly in plastic wrap. Refrigerate at least 1 hour or until firm.

Autumn Apple Bars

1 package (15 ounces)
   refrigerated pie crusts
   (2 crusts)

1 cup graham cracker crumbs

8 tart cooking apples, peeled
   and sliced ¼ inch thick
   (8 cups)

1 cup plus 2 tablespoons
   granulated sugar, divided

2½ teaspoons ground cinnamon,
   divided

¼ teaspoon ground nutmeg

1 egg white

1 cup powdered sugar

1 to 2 tablespoons milk

½ teaspoon vanilla

1. Preheat oven to 350°F. Roll out one pie crust to 15×10-inch rectangle on lightly floured surface. Place on bottom of ungreased 15×10-inch jelly-roll pan.

2. Sprinkle graham cracker crumbs over dough; layer apple slices over crumbs. Combine 1 cup granulated sugar, 1½ teaspoons cinnamon and nutmeg in small bowl; sprinkle over apples.

3. Roll out remaining pie crust to 15×10-inch rectangle; place over apple layer. Beat egg white in small bowl until foamy; brush over top crust. Stir remaining 2 tablespoons granulated sugar and remaining 1 teaspoon cinnamon in separate small bowl; sprinkle over crust. Bake 45 minutes or until lightly browned.

4. Combine powdered sugar, 1 tablespoon milk and vanilla in small bowl. Add additional milk, if necessary, to reach desired consistency. Drizzle over top. Cut into bars.

Makes about 3 dozen bars

Cocoa-Orange-Cranberry Bars

½ cup dried cranberries

2 tablespoons thawed frozen orange juice concentrate

1 cup sugar

½ cup unsweetened cocoa powder

½ cup (1 stick) butter, melted

2 eggs

2 teaspoons grated orange peel

2 teaspoons vanilla

¾ cup all-purpose flour

½ teaspoon baking powder

¼ teaspoon salt

½ cup white chocolate chips

½ cup chopped pecans

1. Preheat oven to 350°F. Grease 9-inch square baking pan.

2. Combine cranberries and orange juice concentrate in medium microwavable bowl. Microwave on HIGH 30 seconds. Cover and let stand 5 minutes.

3. Beat sugar, cocoa and butter in medium bowl until well blended. Add eggs, orange peel and vanilla; beat until well blended. Stir in flour, baking powder and salt just until blended. Stir in cranberry mixture. Spread batter in prepared pan. Sprinkle evenly with chocolate chips and pecans.

4. Bake 30 minutes or until toothpick inserted into center comes out clean. Cool completely in pan on wire rack. Cut into squares.

Makes 12 to 16 bars

Apple Butter Cookies with Penuche Frosting

1 cup (2 sticks) butter, softened
½ cup granulated sugar
½ cup packed brown sugar
1 cup unsweetened apple butter
1 egg
1 teaspoon vanilla
2 cups all-purpose flour
1 teaspoon baking powder
1 teaspoon baking soda

1 teaspoon ground cinnamon
¼ teaspoon salt
¾ cup chopped toasted walnuts* or raisins
Penuche Frosting (page 67)

To toast walnuts, spread in single layer on ungreased baking sheet. Bake in preheated 350°F oven 5 to 7 minutes or until lightly browned, stirring occasionally.

1. Preheat oven to 350°F. Line cookie sheets with parchment paper.

2. Beat butter, granulated sugar and brown sugar with electric mixer on medium speed until creamy. Add apple butter, egg and vanilla; beat until light and fluffy. Gradually add flour, baking powder, baking soda, cinnamon and salt, beating on low speed until well blended; stir in nuts. Drop dough by rounded teaspoonfuls 2 inches apart onto prepared cookie sheets.

3. Bake 10 to 12 minutes or until edges are lightly browned. Remove to wire racks; cool completely.

4. Prepare Penuche Frosting. Frost cookies.

Makes about 4½ dozen cookies

Penuche Frosting

½ cup packed brown sugar
3 tablespoons butter

¼ cup whipping cream
1½ to 2 cups powdered sugar

1. Melt brown sugar and butter in medium saucepan over medium-high heat, stirring frequently. Bring to a boil; cook 1 minute or until slightly thickened, stirring constantly. Remove from heat; cool 10 minutes.

2. Add cream; beat until smooth. Add powdered sugar, ¼ cup at a time, beating well after each addition until frosting is desired consistency.

Chocolate Raspberry Thumbprints

1½ cups (3 sticks) butter, softened

1 cup granulated sugar

1 egg

1 teaspoon vanilla

3 cups all-purpose flour

¼ cup unsweetened cocoa powder

½ teaspoon salt

1 cup mini semisweet chocolate chips (optional)

Powdered sugar (optional)

⅔ cup raspberry jam

1. Preheat oven to 350°F. Line cookie sheets with parchment paper.

2. Beat butter and granulated sugar in large bowl with electric mixer at medium speed. Beat in egg and vanilla until light and fluffy. Mix in flour, cocoa and salt at low speed until well blended. Stir in mini chocolate chips, if desired.

3. Shape level tablespoonfuls of dough into balls. Place 2 inches apart on prepared cookie sheets. Make deep indentation in center of each ball with thumb.

4. Bake 12 to 15 minutes until just set. Cool on cookie sheets 2 minutes. Remove to wire racks; cool completely.

5. Sprinkle cookies with powdered sugar, if desired. Fill centers with jam. Store between layers of waxed paper in airtight containers.

Makes 4½ dozen cookies

TIP: If you're making these cookies as a gift, fill them with jam before baking instead of after. This will set the jam and make the cookies easier to stack and wrap.

Apricot Biscotti

3 cups all-purpose flour
1½ teaspoons baking soda
½ teaspoon salt
3 eggs
⅔ cup sugar
1 teaspoon vanilla

½ cup chopped dried apricots*
⅓ cup sliced almonds, chopped
1 tablespoon milk

*Other chopped dried fruits, such as dried cherries, cranberries or blueberries, can be substituted.

1. Preheat oven to 350°F. Line cookie sheet with parchment paper. Combine flour, baking soda and salt in medium bowl.

2. Beat eggs, sugar and vanilla in large bowl with electric mixer at medium speed until blended. Add flour mixture; beat until well blended.

3. Stir in apricots and almonds. Turn out dough onto lightly floured surface. Knead four to six times. Shape dough into 20-inch log; place on prepared cookie sheet. Brush dough with milk.

4. Bake 30 minutes or until firm. Remove from oven; cool 10 minutes. Cut diagonally into 30 slices. Place slices on cookie sheet. Bake 10 minutes; turn and bake additional 10 minutes. Remove to wire rack; cool completely. Store in airtight container.

Makes 2½ dozen biscotti

GIFT IDEAS: Make several batches of biscotti with a variety of fruit and nut combinations. Dip one end of each cookie into melted white or dark chocolate and sprinkle with toasted chopped almonds or other nuts. Let stand on parchment paper until set. Pack cookies into jars decorative jars or stand the cookies in an extra large mug and wrap with cellophane. Include individually wrapped tea bags, hot chocolate mix or specialty coffee.

Apple-Cranberry Crescent Cookies

1¼ cups chopped fresh apples
½ cup dried cranberries
½ cup sour cream
1 egg
¼ cup (½ stick) butter, melted
3 tablespoons sugar, divided

1 package (¼ ounce) rapid-rise active dry yeast
1 teaspoon vanilla
2 cups all-purpose flour
1 teaspoon ground cinnamon
1 tablespoon milk

1. Preheat oven to 350°F. Line cookie sheets with parchment paper.

2. Place apples and cranberries in food processor; pulse until finely chopped. Set aside.

3. Combine sour cream, egg, butter and 2 tablespoons sugar in medium bowl. Add yeast and vanilla. Add flour; stir to form ball. Turn dough out onto lightly floured work surface. Knead 1 minute. Cover with plastic wrap; let stand 10 minutes.

4. Divide dough into thirds. Roll one portion into 12-inch circle. Spread with one third of apple mixture (about ¼ cup). Cut dough to make eight wedges. Roll up each wedge, beginning at outside edge. Place on prepared cookie sheet; turn ends of cookies to form crescents. Repeat with remaining dough and apple mixture.

5. Combine remaining 1 tablespoon sugar and cinnamon in small bowl. Lightly brush cookies with milk; sprinkle with sugar-cinnamon mixture. Bake 18 to 20 minutes or until lightly browned.

Makes 2 dozen cookies

Chocolate Cherry Cookies

1 package (about 16 ounces) devil's food cake mix

$3/4$ cup ($1^1/2$ sticks) butter, softened

2 eggs

1 teaspoon almond extract

24 maraschino cherries, rinsed, drained and cut into halves

$1/4$ cup white chocolate chips

1 teaspoon canola oil

1. Preheat oven to 350°F. Line cookie sheets with parchment paper.

2. Beat cake mix, butter, eggs and almond extract in large bowl with electric mixer at low speed until crumbly. Beat at medium speed 2 minutes or until smooth dough forms. (Dough will be very sticky.)

3. Shape dough into 1-inch balls. Place 2 inches apart on prepared cookie sheets; flatten slightly. Place 1 cherry half in center of each cookie.

4. Bake 8 to 9 minutes or until cookies are no longer shiny and tops begin to crack. Cool on cookie sheets 2 minutes. Remove to wire racks; cool completely.

5. Place white chocolate chips and oil in small microwavable bowl. Microwave on HIGH 30 seconds; stir. Microwave at additional 30-second intervals, stirring after each interval, until melted and smooth. Drizzle over cookies. Let stand until set.

Makes 4 dozen cookies

Elegant Nibbles

Tea Cookies

1 cup all-purpose flour
$\frac{1}{2}$ cup sugar
2 tablespoons cornstarch
$\frac{1}{8}$ teaspoon salt

2 tablespoons milk
1 teaspoon vanilla
6 tablespoons butter, softened

1. Preheat oven to 350°F. Combine flour, sugar, cornstarch and salt in small bowl; mix well. Stir in milk and vanilla. Cut in butter with pastry blender or two knives until stiff dough forms.

2. Place dough between two sheets of waxed paper; roll to $\frac{1}{8}$-inch thickness. Cut dough using 2-inch cookie cutter; place cutouts 1$\frac{1}{2}$ inches apart on ungreased cookie sheets. Reroll dough scraps and cut out more cookies.

3. Bake 10 to 12 minutes or until edges of cookies are lightly browned. Remove to wire racks; cool completely.

Makes 2 dozen cookies

Black and White Sandwich Cookies

COOKIES

- 1¼ cups (2½ sticks) butter
- ¾ cup superfine or granulated sugar
- 1 egg
- 1½ teaspoons vanilla
- 2⅓ cups all-purpose flour, divided
- ¼ teaspoon salt
- ⅓ cup unsweetened cocoa powder

FILLING

- ½ cup (1 stick) butter
- 4 ounces cream cheese
- 2 cups plus 2 tablespoons powdered sugar
- 2 tablespoons unsweetened cocoa powder

1. For cookies, beat 1¼ cups butter and superfine sugar in large bowl with electric mixer until creamy. Beat in egg and vanilla until well blended. Beat in 2 cups flour and salt at low speed until combined.

2. Remove half of dough to medium bowl; stir in remaining ⅓ cup flour. Add ⅓ cup cocoa to dough in mixer bowl; beat just until blended. Wrap doughs separately in plastic wrap; refrigerate 30 minutes or until firm.

3. Preheat oven to 350°F. Roll out plain dough on floured surface to ¼-inch thickness. Cut out 2-inch circles with round cookie cutters; place 2 inches apart on nonstick cookie sheet. Repeat with chocolate dough.

4. Bake 8 minutes or until firm but not browned. Remove to wire racks; cool completely.

5. For filling, beat ½ cup butter and cream cheese in medium bowl with electric mixer until well blended. Add 2 cups powdered sugar; beat until creamy. Remove half of filling to small bowl; stir in remaining 2 tablespoons powdered sugar. Add 2 tablespoons cocoa to filling in mixer bowl; beat until smooth.

6. Pipe or spread chocolate frosting on flat side of half of plain cookies; top with remaining plain cookies. Pipe or spread vanilla frosting on flat side of half of chocolate cookies; top with remaining chocolate cookies.

Makes 22 to 24 cookies

GIFT IDEAS: Use a 1-inch round cookie cutter to yield twice as many cookies. To make these cookies extra special, dip half of each assembled sandwich cookie into melted bittersweet or semisweet chocolate. Sprinkle with multicolored sprinkles or holiday decors. Let stand on parchment paper until set.

Lemon Drops

2 cups all-purpose flour
⅛ teaspoon salt
1 cup (2 sticks) butter,
softened

1 cup powdered sugar, divided
Grated peel of 1 lemon
2 teaspoons lemon juice

1. Preheat oven to 300°F. Combine flour and salt in medium bowl.

2. Beat butter and ¾ cup powdered sugar in large bowl with electric mixer at medium speed until fluffy. Beat in lemon peel and juice until well blended. Add flour mixture, ½ cup at a time, beating at low speed just until blended after each addition. Shape rounded teaspoonfuls of dough into balls. Place 1 inch apart on ungreased cookie sheets.

3. Bake 20 to 25 minutes or until bottoms are lightly browned. Cool on cookie sheets 5 minutes. Remove to wire racks; cool completely. Sprinkle with remaining ¼ cup powdered sugar.

Makes about 6 dozen cookies

Parmesan and Pine Nut Shortbread

½ cup all-purpose flour
⅓ cup whole wheat flour
⅓ cup cornmeal
¼ teaspoon salt
½ cup (1 stick) butter, softened

½ cup shredded Parmesan cheese
⅓ cup sugar
¼ cup pine nuts

1. Combine all-purpose flour, whole wheat flour, cornmeal and salt in small bowl.

2. Beat butter, cheese and sugar in large bowl with electric mixer at high speed until light and fluffy. Gradually add flour mixture, beating well at low speed after each addition. Turn out dough onto lightly floured surface. Shape into 8- to 10-inch long log 2 inches in diameter. Wrap in plastic wrap; refrigerate 30 minutes.

3. Preheat oven to 375°F. Line cookie sheet with parchment paper. Cut dough into ⅓-inch slices with sharp knife. Place 1 inch apart on prepared cookie sheet. Press 3 to 5 pine nuts on each slice.

4. Bake 11 to 13 minutes or until firm and lightly browned. Cool on cookie sheet 5 minutes. Remove to wire rack; cool completely.

Makes about 2 dozen cookies

Chocolate Strawberry Stackers

Easy All-Purpose Cookie Dough (page 60)
$\frac{1}{2}$ cup semisweet chocolate chips, melted
6 tablespoons butter, softened
$\frac{1}{3}$ cup strawberry jam

$\frac{1}{2}$ teaspoon vanilla
$\frac{1}{4}$ teaspoon salt
2 cups powdered sugar
1 to 2 tablespoons milk (optional)

1. Prepare Easy All-Purpose Cookie Dough through step 1, adding melted chocolate with sugars. Shape dough into 14-inch log. Wrap in plastic wrap; refrigerate 1 hour.

2. Preheat oven to 300°F. Cut log into $\frac{1}{3}$-inch-thick slices; place on ungreased cookie sheets. Bake 15 to 18 minutes or until set. Cool on cookie sheets 5 minutes. Remove to wire racks; cool completely.

3. Beat butter in large bowl with electric mixer at medium speed until smooth. Beat in jam, vanilla and salt until blended. Gradually add powdered sugar; beat until fluffy. If mixture is too thick, gradually beat in milk until desired spreading consistency is reached. Spread frosting over flat sides of half of cookies; top with remaining cookies.

Makes about 20 cookies

Espresso Cookie Cups

1 ounce unsweetened
chocolate, chopped

¼ cup (½ stick) butter

⅓ cup granulated sugar

2 tablespoons instant espresso
powder

1 egg

1 teaspoon vanilla

2 tablespoons cake flour

¼ teaspoon salt

1 package (12 ounces) flaky
biscuit dough

Powdered sugar

1. Preheat oven to 350°F. Spray 24 mini (1-inch) muffin cups with nonstick cooking spray.

2. Melt chocolate and butter in small heavy saucepan over low heat, stirring constantly; remove from heat. Stir in granulated sugar and espresso powder. Whisk in egg and vanilla. Mix in flour and salt.

3. Separate individual biscuits, then pull each biscuit apart horizontally into three pieces each. Press each piece into bottom and up sides of muffin pan. Freeze 10 minutes.

4. Bake 6 minutes or until lightly browned around edges. While still hot, press bottom and sides of biscuits against pan using handle of wood spoon to make well in centers. Fill with chocolate mixture.

5. Bake 7 minutes or until set. Remove to wire racks; cool completely. Dust with powdered sugar just before serving.

Makes 2 dozen cookies

Toffee Creme Sandwich Cookies

1 jar (7 ounces) marshmallow creme

3/4 cup toffee baking bits, divided

16 (2-inch) shortbread cookies

1. Combine marshmallow creme and 1/4 cup toffee bits in medium bowl until well blended. (Mixture will be stiff.)

2. Spoon 1 teaspoon marshmallow mixture onto flat side of 1 cookie. Top with another cookie, flat side down. Roll edges in remaining 1/2 cup toffee bits. Repeat with remaining marshmallow creme mixture, cookies and toffee bits.

Makes 8 cookies

TIP: This recipe can easily be doubled or tripled. Use store-bought cookies or make your own. Try Refrigerator Cookies (page 34) or Easy All-Purpose Cookie Dough (page 60), rolled into a log, cut into 1/4-inch slices and baked at 300°F 15 minutes or until set but not browned.

Ginger Polenta Cookies

2¼ cups all-purpose flour

½ cup uncooked instant polenta or yellow cornmeal

½ cup toasted pistachio nuts or pine nuts,* finely chopped

½ cup dried cranberries, finely chopped

¼ teaspoon salt

1 cup (2 sticks) butter, softened

¾ cup sugar

1 egg

1 egg yolk

½ cup finely chopped crystallized ginger

½ teaspoon ground ginger

To toast nuts, place in single layer on ungreased baking sheet. Bake in preheated 350°F oven 8 to 10 minutes or until lightly browned, stirring occasionally.

1. Combine flour, polenta, nuts, cranberries and salt in medium bowl.

2. Beat butter and sugar in large bowl with electric mixer at medium speed until light and fluffy. Beat in egg, egg yolk, crystallized ginger and ground ginger. Add flour mixture; mix at low speed until well blended.

3. Shape dough into ball; divide in half. Roll into two 9-inch logs; wrap in plastic wrap. Roll logs to smooth surface, if necessary. Refrigerate 4 to 6 hours or until firm.

4. Preheat oven to 300°F. Line cookie sheets with parchment paper. Cut logs into ¼-inch slices; place cookies on prepared cookie sheets.

5. Bake 15 to 18 minutes or until edges are golden. Cool on cookie sheets 2 to 3 minutes. Remove to wire racks; cool completely.

Makes about 5 dozen cookies

Chocolate Hazelnut Sandwich Cookies

3/4 cup (1 1/2 sticks) butter, softened

3/4 cup sugar

3 egg yolks

1 teaspoon vanilla

2 cups all-purpose flour

1/4 teaspoon salt

2/3 cup chocolate hazelnut spread

1. Beat butter and sugar in large bowl with electric mixer at medium speed 1 minute. Beat in egg yolks and vanilla until well blended. Add flour and salt; beat at low speed just until combined. Divide dough in half. Shape each piece into 6-inch-long log 1 1/2 inches in diameter. Wrap in plastic wrap; refrigerate at least 2 hours or until firm.

2. Preheat oven to 350°F. Line cookie sheets with parchment paper. Cut dough into 1/8-inch-thick slices; place 1 inch apart on prepared cookie sheets.

3. Bake 10 to 12 minutes or until edges are light brown. Cool on cookie sheets 5 minutes. Remove to wire racks; cool completely.

4. Spread 1 teaspoon hazelnut spread on flat side of half of cookies; top with remaining cookies. Store covered in airtight container.

Makes 2 1/2 dozen cookies

Rosemary Honey Shortbread Cookies

2 cups all-purpose flour

1 tablespoon fresh rosemary leaves,* minced

1/2 teaspoon salt

1/2 teaspoon baking powder

3/4 cup (11/2 sticks) butter, softened

1/2 cup powdered sugar

2 tablespoons honey

*For best flavor, use only fresh rosemary or substitute fresh or dried lavender buds.

1. Combine flour, rosemary, salt and baking powder in medium bowl.

2. Beat butter, powdered sugar and honey in large bowl with electric mixer at medium speed until creamy. Beat in flour mixture at low speed just until blended. (Mixture will be crumbly.) Shape dough into log. Wrap in plastic wrap; refrigerate 1 hour or until firm. (Dough can be refrigerated several days before baking.)

3. Preheat oven to 350°F. Line cookie sheets with parchment paper. Cut log into 1/2-inch slices. Place 2 inches apart on prepared cookie sheets.

4. Bake 13 minutes or until set. Cool on cookie sheets 1 minute. Remove to wire racks; cool completely.

Makes 2 dozen cookies

Chocolate Almond Meringue Sandwich Cookies

½ cup sugar, divided

¼ cup ground almonds

1 tablespoon unsweetened cocoa powder

1 teaspoon cornstarch

2 egg whites

⅛ teaspoon cream of tartar

¼ teaspoon almond extract

⅓ cup chocolate fudge topping

1. Preheat oven to 250°F. Line cookie sheets with foil; spray foil with nonstick cooking spray. Combine 3 tablespoons sugar, almonds, cocoa and cornstarch in small bowl.

2. Beat egg whites in medium bowl with electric mixer at medium speed until foamy. Add cream of tartar; beat at high speed until soft peaks form. Gradually add almond extract and remaining sugar; beat at high speed until stiff peaks form. Gently fold cocoa mixture into egg whites.

3. Drop rounded teaspoonfuls of meringue mixture about 2 inches apart onto prepared cookie sheets. (Or mixture may be piped using piping bag fitted with large tip.)

4. Bake 40 minutes. Cool cookies on cookie sheets 2 minutes; use thin spatula to loosen cookies from foil. Remove to wire racks; cool completely.

5. Spread 1 teaspoon fudge topping on flat side of half of cookies; top with remaining cookies. Store cookies in airtight container up to 2 days.

Makes 15 cookies

Buttery Lemongrass Wedges

1 cup sliced almonds with
skins, toasted and cooled

³/₄ cup superfine or granulated
sugar

¹/₄ cup lemongrass purée*

Grated peel of 2 large lemons

¹/₂ teaspoon salt

1¹/₄ cups all-purpose flour

³/₄ cup (1¹/₂ sticks) cold butter,
cut into small pieces

2 teaspoons vanilla

Powdered sugar (optional)

*Lemongrass purée can be found in
the refrigerated produce section of
well-stocked supermarkets or at Asian
specialty markets.*

1. Pulse almonds in food processor. Add sugar, lemongrass, lemon peel and salt; pulse until finely ground. Add flour; pulse until combined. Add butter and vanilla. Pulse just until large clumps form. *Do not overprocess.*

2. Spray two 9-inch springform pans with nonstick cooking spray. Divide dough in half and pat evenly into pans. Cover with plastic wrap; refrigerate 3 to 4 hours or overnight.

3. Preheat oven to 325°F. Bake 20 to 23 minutes or until golden brown. Cool 10 minutes. Remove sides of springform pans and cut each circle into 12 wedges. Cool completely. Sprinkle with powdered sugar, if desired.

Makes 2 dozen cookies

Mini Lemon Sandwich Cookies

2 cups all-purpose flour

1¼ cups (2½ sticks) butter, softened, divided

½ cup granulated sugar, divided

⅓ cup whipping cream

1 teaspoon grated lemon peel

⅛ teaspoon lemon extract

¾ cup powdered sugar

2 to 3 teaspoons lemon juice

1 teaspoon vanilla

Yellow food coloring (optional)

1. For cookies, combine flour, 1 cup butter, ¼ cup granulated sugar, cream, lemon peel and lemon extract in large bowl. Beat with electric mixer at medium speed 2 to 3 minutes or until well blended. Divide dough into thirds. Wrap each piece in waxed paper; refrigerate until firm.

2. Preheat oven to 375°F. Place remaining ¼ cup granulated sugar in shallow bowl. Roll out each piece of dough to ⅛-inch thickness on floured surface. Cut out dough with 1½-inch round cookie cutter. Dip both sides of each cookie in sugar. Place 1 inch apart on ungreased cookie sheets; pierce several times with fork.

3. Bake 6 to 9 minutes or until cookies are slightly puffed but not brown. Cool on cookie sheets 1 minute. Remove to wire racks; cool completely.

4. For filling, beat powdered sugar, remaining ¼ cup butter, lemon juice and vanilla in large bowl with electric mixer at medium speed 1 to 2 minutes or until smooth. Tint with food coloring, if desired. Spread ½ teaspoon filling each on flat side of half of cookies; top with remaining cookies.

Makes 4½ dozen cookies

Yuletide Bars and Brownies

Toffee Bars

½ cup (1 stick) butter, softened
½ cup packed brown sugar
1 egg yolk
1 teaspoon vanilla

1 cup all-purpose flour
1 cup milk chocolate chips
½ cup chopped walnuts or pecans

1. Preheat oven to 350°F. Spray 13×9-inch baking pan with nonstick cooking spray.

2. Beat butter and brown sugar in large bowl with electric mixer at medium speed until creamy. Blend in egg yolk and vanilla. Stir in flour until well blended. Press dough into prepared pan.

3. Bake 15 minutes or until golden. Sprinkle evenly with chocolate chips. Let stand several minutes until chips melt; spread chocolate evenly over bars. Sprinkle with walnuts. Score into bars while still warm. Cool completely in pan on wire rack; cut into bars along score lines.

Makes 2 to 3 dozen bars

Chocolate Chip Sour Cream Brownies

½ cup (1 stick) butter, softened
1 cup packed brown sugar
1 cup sour cream
1 egg
1 teaspoon vanilla
½ cup unsweetened cocoa powder
½ teaspoon baking soda
¼ teaspoon salt
2 cups all-purpose flour
1 cup semisweet chocolate chips
Powdered sugar (optional)

1. Preheat oven to 350°F. Spray 13×9-inch baking pan with nonstick cooking spray.

2. Beat butter and brown sugar in large bowl with electric mixer until creamy. Add sour cream, egg and vanilla; beat until light and fluffy. Add cocoa, baking soda and salt; beat until smooth. Gradually beat in flour at low speed until well blended. Stir in chocolate chips. Spread batter evenly in prepared pan.

3. Bake 25 to 30 minutes or until toothpick inserted into center comes out clean and center springs back when touched. Cool completely in pan on wire rack. Sprinkle with powdered sugar, if desired. Cut into bars.

Makes 2 to 3 dozen brownies

Chocolate Caramel Bars

2 cups all-purpose flour
1½ cups packed brown sugar, divided
1¼ cups (2½ sticks) butter, softened, divided

1 cup chopped pecans
1 cup semisweet chocolate chips

1. Preheat oven to 350°F.

2. Combine flour, 1 cup brown sugar and ½ cup butter in large bowl until crumbly. Press firmly into 13×9-inch baking pan; sprinkle pecans evenly over top.

3. Combine remaining ½ cup brown sugar and ¾ cup butter in medium heavy saucepan. Cook over medium heat until mixture comes to a boil, stirring constantly. Boil 1 minute, stirring constantly. Pour caramel evenly over pecans and crust.

4. Bake 18 to 20 minutes or until caramel layer bubbles evenly all over. Immediately sprinkle with chocolate chips. Let stand 2 minutes or until chips melt; spread chocolate evenly over bars. Let stand until chocolate is set; cut into bars.

Makes 2 to 3 dozen bars

Caramel Bacon Nut Brownies

¾ cup (1½ sticks) butter

4 ounces unsweetened chocolate, chopped

2 cups sugar

4 eggs

1 cup all-purpose flour

1 package (14 ounces) caramels

¼ cup whipping cream

2 cups pecan halves or coarsely chopped pecans, divided

4 slices bacon, crisp-cooked and crumbled

1 package (12 ounces) chocolate chunks or chips, divided

1. Preheat oven to 350°F. Spray 13×9-inch baking pan with nonstick cooking spray.

2. Place butter and chocolate in large microwavable bowl. Microwave on HIGH 1½ to 2 minutes or until melted and smooth, stirring at 30-second intervals. Stir in sugar. Add eggs, one at a time, beating until blended after each addition. Stir in flour. Spread half of batter in prepared pan. Bake 20 minutes.

3. Meanwhile, combine caramels and cream in medium microwavable bowl. Microwave on HIGH 1½ to 2 minutes or until caramels begin to melt; stir until smooth. Stir in 1 cup pecan halves and bacon.

4. Spread caramel mixture over partially baked brownie layer. Sprinkle with half of chocolate chunks. Pour remaining brownie batter over top; sprinkle with remaining 1 cup pecan halves and chocolate chunks. Bake 25 minutes or until set. Cool completely in pan on wire rack. Cut into squares.

Makes 2 to 3 dozen brownies

O'Henrietta Bars

Cooking Spray
½ cup (1 stick) butter or margarine, softened
½ cup packed brown sugar
½ cup KARO® Light or Dark Corn Syrup

1 teaspoon vanilla
3 cups quick oats, uncooked
½ cup (3 ounces) semisweet chocolate chips
¼ cup creamy peanut butter

1. Preheat oven to 350°F. Spray 8- or 9-inch square baking pan with cooking spray.

2. Beat butter, brown sugar, corn syrup and vanilla in large bowl with mixer at medium speed until smooth. Stir in oats. Press into prepared pan.

3. Bake 25 minutes or until center is barely firm. Cool on wire rack 5 minutes.

4. Sprinkle with chocolate chips; top with small spoonfuls of peanut butter. Let stand 5 minutes; spread peanut butter and chocolate over bars, swirling to marble.

5. Cool completely on wire rack before cutting. Cut into bars; refrigerate 15 minutes to set topping.

Makes 24 bars

PREP TIME: 20 minutes
BAKE TIME: 25 minutes, plus cooling

White Chocolate Peppermint Brownies

BROWNIES

1 package (12 ounces) white chocolate chips, divided

¼ cup granulated sugar

3 eggs

1 cup all-purpose flour

½ cup (1 stick) butter, softened

½ teaspoon salt

½ cup chopped peppermint candies

FROSTING

1¼ cups powdered sugar

6 tablespoons butter, softened

3 tablespoons cream cheese

Crushed peppermint candies

1. Preheat oven to 350°F. Spray 9-inch square baking pan with nonstick cooking spray.

2. Melt half of white chocolate chips in small saucepan over very low heat, stirring constantly until smooth. Cool slightly.

3. Beat granulated sugar and eggs in large bowl with electric mixer at medium-high speed 5 minutes. Add melted chocolate, flour, ½ cup butter and salt; beat on low speed until blended. Stir in chopped peppermints. Spread batter in prepared pan.

4. Bake 20 to 25 minutes or until toothpick inserted into center comes out clean. Cool completely in pan on wire rack.

5. Meanwhile for frosting, melt remaining half of white chocolate chips in small saucepan over very low heat, stirring constantly until smooth. Cool slightly. Beat powdered sugar, 6 tablespoons butter and cream cheese and in large bowl with electric mixer until smooth. Beat in melted chocolate. Spread over brownies; sprinkle with crushed peppermint candies.

Makes 12 to 16 brownies

Tangy Lemon Raspberry Bars

³/₄ cup packed brown sugar
¹/₂ cup (1 stick) butter, softened
Grated peel of 1 lemon
1 cup all-purpose flour
1 cup old-fashioned oats

1 teaspoon baking powder
¹/₂ teaspoon salt
¹/₂ cup raspberry jam

1. Preheat oven to 350°F. Spray 8-inch square baking pan with nonstick cooking spray.

2. Beat brown sugar, butter and lemon peel in large bowl with electric mixer at medium speed until combined. Add flour, oats, baking powder and salt; beat at low speed until combined. Reserve ¹/₄ cup mixture. Press remaining mixture into prepared pan. Spread jam over top; sprinkle with reserved mixture.

3. Bake 25 minutes or until edges are lightly browned. Cool completely in pan on wire rack. Cut into bars.

Makes 12 to 16 bars

Hawaiian Bars

1⅓ cups all-purpose flour

1 teaspoon baking powder

¼ teaspoon baking soda

¼ teaspoon salt

10 tablespoons (1¼ sticks) butter

1 teaspoon vanilla

2 eggs

1 cup packed dark brown sugar

¾ cup coarsely chopped salted macadamia nuts

¾ cup flaked coconut

⅓ cup granulated sugar

1. Preheat oven to 350°F. Spray 9-inch square baking pan with nonstick cooking spray. Whisk flour, baking powder, baking soda and salt in medium bowl.

2. Melt butter in large heavy saucepan over low heat. Remove from heat; stir in vanilla. Beat in eggs, one at a time. Add flour mixture, brown sugar, nuts, coconut and granulated sugar; mix well. Spread batter in prepared pan.

3. Bake 30 minutes or until edges begin to pull away from sides of pan. Cool completely in pan on wire rack. Cut into bars. Store in airtight container.

Makes 12 to 16 bars

NOTE: Bars firm up and taste even better the day after they're made.

Fruit and Pecan Brownies

2 ounces unsweetened
  chocolate, chopped
1 cup sugar
½ cup (1 stick) butter, softened
2 eggs
1 teaspoon vanilla
1 cup chopped dried mixed
  fruit

½ cup all-purpose flour
1 cup coarsely chopped
  pecans, divided
1 cup semisweet chocolate
  chips, divided

1. Preheat oven to 350°F. Spray 8-inch square baking pan with nonstick cooking spray. Melt unsweetened chocolate in top of double boiler over simmering water. Remove from heat; cool slightly.

2. Beat sugar and butter in large bowl with electric mixer at medium speed until light and fluffy. Add eggs, one at a time, beating until blended after each addition. Beat in chocolate and vanilla. Stir in fruit, flour, ½ cup pecans and ½ cup chocolate chips. Spread batter in prepared pan. Sprinkle with remaining ½ cup pecans and ½ cup chocolate chips.

3. Bake 25 to 30 minutes or just until center feels firm. *Do not overbake.* Remove from oven; cover warm bars with waxed paper or foil. Cool completely in pan on wire rack. Cut into squares.

Makes 12 to 16 brownies

Cherry
Cheesecake Swirl Bars

1²/₃ cups shortbread cookie
crumbs
¹/₂ cup (1 stick) butter, melted
³/₄ cup sugar, divided
2 packages (8 ounces each)
cream cheese, softened

3 eggs
¹/₂ cup sour cream
¹/₂ teaspoon almond extract
3 tablespoons strained cherry
preserves, melted

1. Preheat oven to 325°F.

2. Combine cookie crumbs, butter and ¹/₄ cup sugar in medium bowl; mix well. Press mixture into 9-inch square baking pan. Bake 10 minutes or until set but not browned. Cool completely.

3. Beat cream cheese in large bowl with electric mixer at medium speed until fluffy. Add remaining ¹/₂ cup sugar; beat until smooth. Add eggs, one at a time, beating well after each addition. Add sour cream and almond extract; beat until well blended. Spread evenly in prepared crust.

4. Drizzle melted preserves over cheesecake batter. Drag tip of knife through jam and batter to swirl.

5. Place pan in 13×9-inch baking dish; add water to come halfway up sides of cheesecake.

6. Bake 45 to 50 minutes or until knife inserted 1 inch from edge comes out clean. Cool completely in pan on wire rack. Cover and refrigerate 2 hours or until ready to serve.

Makes 12 to 16 bars

Dulce de Leche Blondies

2 cups all-purpose flour
1 teaspoon baking soda
1 teaspoon salt
1 cup (2 sticks) butter,
softened

1 cup packed brown sugar
2 eggs
1½ teaspoons vanilla
1 package (14 ounces) caramels
½ cup evaporated milk

1. Preheat oven to 350°F. Spray 13×9-inch baking pan with nonstick cooking spray. Whisk flour, baking soda and salt in medium bowl.

2. Beat butter and brown sugar in large bowl with electric mixer at medium speed until creamy. Add eggs, one at a time, beating well after each addition. Beat in vanilla. Gradually add flour mixture; beat just until blended. Spread half of batter in prepared pan. Bake 8 minutes. Cool in pan on wire rack 5 minutes.

3. Meanwhile, melt caramels with evaporated milk in small saucepan over low heat; reserve 2 tablespoons. Pour remaining caramel mixture over baked bottom layer. Drop tablespoonfuls of remaining batter over caramel layer; swirl slightly with knife.

4. Bake 25 minutes or until golden brown. Cool completely in pan on wire rack. Cut into squares. Reheat reserved caramel, if necessary; drizzle over bars.

Makes 2 to 3 dozen bars

Shortbread Turtle Cookie Bars

1¼ cups (2½ sticks) butter, softened, divided

1 cup all-purpose flour

1 cup old-fashioned oats

1½ cups packed brown sugar, divided

1 teaspoon ground cinnamon

¼ teaspoon salt

1½ cups chopped pecans

6 ounces bittersweet or semisweet chocolate, finely chopped

4 ounces white chocolate, finely chopped

1. Preheat oven to 350°F.

2. Beat ½ cup butter with electric mixer at medium speed 2 minutes or until light and fluffy. Add flour, oats, ¾ cup brown sugar, cinnamon and salt; beat at low speed until coarse crumbs form. Press firmly into ungreased 13×9-inch baking pan.

3. Combine remaining ¾ cup butter and ¾ cup brown sugar in heavy medium saucepan. Cook over medium heat, stirring constantly until mixture comes to a boil. Boil 1 minute without stirring. Remove from heat; stir in pecans. Pour evenly over crust.

4. Bake 18 to 22 minutes or until caramel begins to bubble. Immediately sprinkle with bittersweet and white chocolates; let stand 1 minute or until softened. Swirl with knife. Cool completely in pan on wire rack; cut into bars.

Makes 2 to 3 dozen bars

Chewy Peanut Butter Brownies

¾ cup (1½ sticks) butter, melted

¾ cup creamy peanut butter

1¾ cups sugar

2 teaspoons vanilla

4 eggs, lightly beaten

1¼ cups all-purpose flour

½ teaspoon baking powder

¼ teaspoon salt

¼ cup unsweetened cocoa powder

1. Preheat oven to 350°F. Spray 13×9-inch baking pan with nonstick cooking spray.

2. Beat butter and peanut butter in large bowl with electric mixer at low speed 3 minutes or until well blended. Add sugar and vanilla; beat until blended. Add eggs, one at a time, beating until well blended after each addition. Stir in flour, baking powder and salt just until blended. Reserve 1¾ cups batter. Stir cocoa into remaining batter.

3. Spread chocolate batter in prepared pan. Top with reserved batter. Bake 30 minutes or until edges begin to pull away from sides of pan. Cool completely in pan on wire rack. Cut into bars.

Makes 2 to 3 dozen brownies

International Cheer

Chinese Almond Cookies

1 package (about 16 ounces)
yellow cake mix
5 tablespoons butter, melted
1 egg

1½ teaspoons almond extract
30 whole almonds
1 egg yolk
1 teaspoon water

1. Beat cake mix, butter, egg and almond extract in large bowl with electric mixer at medium speed until well blended. Shape dough into disc. Wrap in plastic wrap; refrigerate 4 hours or overnight.

2. Preheat oven to 350°F. Line cookie sheets with parchment paper.

3. Shape dough into 1-inch balls; place 2 inches apart on prepared cookie sheets. Press 1 almond into center of each ball, flattening slightly. Whisk egg yolk and water in small bowl. Brush tops of cookies with egg yolk mixture.

4. Bake 10 to 12 minutes or until lightly browned. Cool on cookie sheets 5 minutes. Remove to wire racks; cool completely.

Makes about 2½ dozen cookies

Chocolate-Frosted Lebkuchen

1 cup sugar

4 eggs

1½ cups all-purpose flour

1 cup (6 ounces) ground almonds*

⅓ cup candied lemon peel, finely chopped

⅓ cup candied orange peel, finely chopped

1½ teaspoons ground cinnamon

1 teaspoon grated lemon peel

½ teaspoon ground cardamom

½ teaspoon ground nutmeg

¼ teaspoon ground cloves

3 ounces bittersweet or semisweet chocolate, coarsely chopped

1 tablespoon butter

*To grind almonds, place in food processor or blender. Pulse until finely ground but not pasty.

1. Beat sugar and eggs in large bowl with electric mixer at high speed 10 minutes.

2. Meanwhile, combine flour, almonds, candied lemon and orange peels, cinnamon, grated lemon peel, cardamom, nutmeg and cloves in another large bowl. Add egg mixture; stir until well blended. Cover; refrigerate 12 hours or overnight.

3. Preheat oven to 350°F. Line cookie sheets with parchment paper. Drop dough by rounded teaspoonfuls 2 inches apart onto prepared cookie sheets. Bake 8 to 10 minutes or just until browned. *Do not overbake.* Remove to wire racks; cool slightly.

4. Meanwhile, combine chocolate and butter in small microwavable bowl. Microwave on HIGH 30 seconds; stir. Repeat until chocolate is melted and mixture is smooth. Spread over tops of warm cookies. Let stand until glaze is set. Store in airtight container.

Makes about 5 dozen cookies

Argentinean
Caramel-Filled Crescents (Pasteles)

3 cups all-purpose flour
½ cup powdered sugar
1 teaspoon baking powder
¼ teaspoon salt
1 cup (2 sticks) butter, cut into small pieces
6 to 7 tablespoons ice water

½ package (14 ounces) caramels
2 tablespoons milk
½ cup flaked coconut
1 egg
1 tablespoon water

1. Combine flour, powdered sugar, baking powder and salt in large bowl. Cut in butter with pastry blender or two knives until mixture forms pea-sized pieces. Add water, 1 tablespoon at a time; toss with fork until mixture holds together. Divide dough in half. Wrap separately in plastic wrap; refrigerate 30 minutes or until firm.

2. Meanwhile, melt caramels and milk in medium saucepan over low heat, stirring constantly; stir in coconut. Remove from heat; cool.

3. Roll out dough on lightly floured surface to ¼-inch thickness. Cut dough with 3-inch round cookie cutter. Gather and reroll scraps; cut additional circles.

4. Preheat oven to 400°F. Line cookie sheets with parchment paper. Beat egg and water in cup. Place ½ teaspoon caramel mixture in center of each dough round. Moisten edge of dough round with egg mixture. Fold dough in half; press edges firmly to seal in filling. Press edges with fork. Place crescents on prepared cookie sheets; brush with egg mixture. Cut 3 slashes across top of each cookie with tip of knife.

5. Bake 15 to 20 minutes or until golden brown. Remove cookies to wire racks; cool completely. Store tightly covered at room temperature.

Makes about 4 dozen cookies

Quebec Maple-Pecan Drops

COOKIES

 1 cup all-purpose flour
 $1/2$ teaspoon baking soda
 $1/4$ teaspoon salt
 $1/2$ cup (1 stick) butter, softened
 $1/2$ cup granulated sugar
 3 tablespoons maple syrup
 1 cup quick oats*
 $1/2$ cup coarsely chopped
    pecans, toasted**
 $1/4$ cup chopped pitted dates

FROSTING (OPTIONAL)

 2 ounces cream cheese,
    softened
 2 tablespoons butter, softened
 2 tablespoons maple syrup
 $1^1/2$ cups sifted powdered sugar
 $1/3$ cup finely chopped pecans,
    toasted

Do not use old-fashioned oats.

**To toast pecans, spread in single layer on baking sheet. Bake in preheated 350°F oven 5 to 7 minutes or until lightly toasted, stirring frequently.*

1. Preheat oven to 350°F. Combine flour, baking soda and salt in medium bowl.

2. Beat $1/2$ cup butter and granulated sugar in large bowl with electric mixer at medium speed until creamy. Beat in 3 tablespoons syrup. Gradually beat in flour mixture, oats, coarsely chopped pecans and dates at low speed. Drop dough by rounded tablespoonfuls 2 inches apart onto ungreased cookie sheets.

3. Bake 12 minutes or until cookies are golden brown. Cool on cookie sheets 2 minutes. Remove to wire racks; cool completely.

4. For frosting, beat cream cheese and 2 tablespoons butter in large bowl with electric mixer at medium speed until smooth. Beat in 2 tablespoons syrup. Gradually beat in powdered sugar until smooth. Spread frosting over cooled cookies; top with finely chopped pecans.

Makes about 2 dozen cookies

Molded Scottish Shortbread

1½ cups all-purpose flour

¼ teaspoon salt

¾ cup (1½ sticks) butter, softened

⅓ cup sugar

1 egg

1. Preheat oven to temperature recommended by shortbread mold manufacturer. Spray 10-inch ceramic shortbread mold with nonstick cooking spray.

2. Combine flour and salt in medium bowl. Beat butter and sugar in large bowl with electric mixer at medium speed until light and fluffy. Add egg; beat until well blended. Gradually add flour mixture; beat at low speed until blended. Press dough firmly into mold.

3. Bake, cool and remove from mold according to manufacturer's directions.

Makes 1 shortbread mold

NOTE: If you don't have a shortbread mold, bake the shortbread as individual cookies instead. Preheat oven to 350°F. Shape dough into 1-inch balls. Place 2 inches apart on ungreased cookie sheets; press with fork to flatten. Bake 18 to 20 minutes or until edges are lightly browned. Cool cookies on cookie sheets 2 minutes. Remove to wire racks; cool completely. Makes 2 dozen cookies.

Welsh Tea Cakes

³/₄ cup chopped dried mixed fruit, fruit bits or golden raisins

2 tablespoons brandy or cognac

2¹/₄ cups all-purpose flour

2¹/₂ teaspoons ground cinnamon, divided

1 teaspoon baking powder

¹/₂ teaspoon baking soda

¹/₄ teaspoon salt

¹/₄ teaspoon ground cloves

1 cup (2 sticks) butter, softened

1¹/₄ cups sugar, divided

1 egg

¹/₃ cup sliced almonds (optional)

1. Preheat oven to 375°F. Combine dried fruit and brandy in medium bowl; let sit at least 10 minutes to plump.

2. Combine flour, 1¹/₂ teaspoons cinnamon, baking powder, baking soda, salt and cloves in medium bowl.

3. Beat butter and 1 cup sugar in large bowl with electric mixer at medium speed until light and fluffy. Beat in egg. Gradually add flour mixture at low speed until well blended. Stir in fruit and brandy mixture with spoon.

4. Combine remaining ¹/₄ cup sugar and 1 teaspoon cinnamon in small bowl. Shape heaping teaspoonfuls of dough into 1-inch balls; roll balls in cinnamon-sugar to coat. Place balls 2 inches apart on ungreased cookie sheets.

5. Press balls to ¹/₄-inch thickness using bottom of glass dipped in granulated sugar. Press 3 almond slices into center of each cookie, if desired.

6. Bake 10 to 12 minutes or until lightly browned. Remove to wire racks; cool completely. Store tightly covered at room temperature or freeze up to 3 months.

Makes about 3¹/₂ dozen cookies

Bolivian Almond Cookies
(Alfajores de Almendras)

4 cups whole almonds

1 cup all-purpose flour

1/4 teaspoon salt

1 cup sugar

3/4 cup (1 1/2 sticks) butter, softened

1 teaspoon vanilla

1/2 teaspoon almond extract

2 eggs

2 tablespoons milk

1 tablespoon grated lemon peel

1 cup sliced almonds

1. Preheat oven to 350°F. Line cookie sheets with parchment paper.

2. Place whole almonds in food processor. Pulse until almonds are ground but not pasty.

3. Combine ground almonds, flour and salt in medium bowl.

4. Beat sugar, butter, vanilla and almond extract in large bowl with electric mixer at medium speed until light and fluffy. Beat in eggs and milk. Gradually add half of flour mixture at low speed until well blended. Stir in lemon peel and remaining flour mixture.

5. Drop rounded teaspoonfuls of dough 2 inches apart onto prepared cookie sheets. Flatten slightly with spoon; top with sliced almonds.

6. Bake 10 to 12 minutes or until edges are lightly browned. Remove to wire racks; cool completely.

Makes about 3 dozen cookies

Belgian Tuile Cookies

½ cup (1 stick) butter, softened
½ cup sugar
1 egg white
1 teaspoon vanilla
¼ teaspoon salt

½ cup all-purpose flour
4 ounces bittersweet chocolate, chopped or semisweet chocolate chips

1. Preheat oven to 375°F. Line cookie sheets with parchment paper.

2. Beat butter and sugar in large bowl with electric mixer at medium speed until light and fluffy. Beat in egg white, vanilla and salt. Gradually add flour at low speed until well blended. Drop rounded teaspoonfuls of batter 4 inches apart onto prepared cookie sheets. (Bake only 4 cookies per sheet.) Flatten slightly with spatula.

3. Bake 6 to 8 minutes or until cookies are deep golden brown. Let cookies stand on cookie sheet 1 minute. Working quickly while cookies are still hot, drape cookies over rolling pin or bottle to form saddle shape; cool completely.

4. Melt chocolate in small heavy saucepan over low heat, stirring constantly.

5. Tilt saucepan to pool chocolate at one end; dip edge of each cookie, turning slowly so entire edge is tinged with chocolate.

6. Transfer cookies to waxed paper; let stand at room temperature 1 hour or until set. Store tightly covered at room temperature. Do not freeze.

Makes about 2½ dozen cookies

Festive Lebkuchen

3 tablespoons butter
1 cup packed brown sugar
¼ cup honey
1 egg
   Grated peel and juice of
   1 lemon

3 cups all-purpose flour
2 teaspoons ground allspice
½ teaspoon baking soda
½ teaspoon salt
   White decorating icing

1. Combine butter, brown sugar and honey in medium saucepan; cook over low heat until butter is melted, stirring constantly. Pour into large bowl; cool 30 minutes.

2. Add egg, lemon peel and lemon juice; beat 2 minutes with electric mixer at high speed. Stir in flour, allspice, baking soda and salt until well blended. Cover; refrigerate overnight or up to 3 days.

3. Preheat oven to 350°F. Line cookie sheets with parchment paper. Roll out dough to ½-inch thickness on lightly floured surface with lightly floured rolling pin. Cut dough with desired cookie cutters; place on prepared cookie sheets.

4. Bake 15 to 18 minutes until edges are lightly browned. Cool on cookie sheets 1 minute. Remove to wire racks; cool completely. Decorate with white frosting. Store in airtight container.

Makes 2 dozen cookies

Old World Pfeffernüsse Cookies

¾ cup packed brown sugar
½ cup (1 stick) butter, softened
½ cup molasses
1 egg
1 tablespoon licorice-flavored liqueur (optional)
3¼ cups all-purpose flour

1 teaspoon baking soda
1 teaspoon ground cinnamon
½ teaspoon ground cloves
¼ teaspoon ground nutmeg
Dash black pepper
Powdered sugar (optional)

1. Preheat oven to 350°F. Line cookie sheets with parchment paper.

2. Beat brown sugar and butter in large bowl with electric mixer at medium speed until creamy. Beat in molasses, egg and liqueur, if desired, until light and fluffy. Mix in flour, baking soda, cinnamon, cloves, nutmeg and pepper at low speed until well blended. Shape level tablespoonfuls of dough into balls. Place 2 inches apart on prepared cookie sheets.

3. Bake 12 to 14 minutes or until set. Cool on cookie sheets 2 minutes. Remove to wire racks; cool completely. Sprinkle with powdered sugar, if desired. Store in airtight containers.

Makes about 4 dozen cookies

Hungarian Lemon Poppy Seed Cookies

1¼ cups all-purpose flour
½ teaspoon baking soda
¼ teaspoon salt
⅔ cup granulated sugar
½ cup (1 stick) butter, softened

1 egg
2 teaspoons grated lemon peel
1 tablespoon poppy seeds
1 cup powdered sugar
2 tablespoons lemon juice

1. Preheat oven to 350°F. Combine flour, baking soda and salt in medium bowl.

2. For cookies, beat granulated sugar and butter in large bowl of electric mixer at medium speed until creamy. Beat in egg and lemon peel. Gradually add flour mixture and poppy seeds at low speed. Drop dough by heaping teaspoonfuls 2 inches apart onto ungreased cookie sheets.

3. Bake 11 to 12 minutes or until edges are lightly browned. Cool on cookie sheets 1 minute. Remove to wire racks; cool completely.

4. For glaze, combine powdered sugar and lemon juice in small bowl; mix well. Drizzle glaze over cookies; let stand about 20 minutes or until glaze is set.

Makes about 2 dozen cookies

Pebbernodders

3 cups all-purpose flour
1 teaspoon baking powder
1 teaspoon ground cinnamon
½ teaspoon ground ginger
½ teaspoon ground cloves
1½ cups sugar

1½ cups (3 sticks) butter, softened
3 eggs
2 teaspoons freshly grated lemon peel

1. Combine flour, baking powder, cinnamon, ginger and cloves in medium bowl.

2. Beat sugar and butter in large bowl with electric mixer at medium speed until creamy. Add eggs and lemon peel; beat until well blended. Gradually add flour mixture at low speed just until blended.

3. Line cookie sheets with parchment paper. Divide dough into four equal pieces; shape each piece into ³/₄-inch-thick rope about 12 inches long. Place ropes on prepared cookie sheets. Freeze about 30 minutes or until firm.

4. Preheat oven to 375°F. Cut frozen ropes into ¼-inch-thick slices; place 1 inch apart on prepared cookie sheets. Bake 10 to 12 minutes or until lightly browned. Remove to wire racks; cool completely.

Makes about 16 dozen small cookies

Hazelnut Biscotti

4 cups all-purpose flour

2 cups sugar

4 teaspoons baking powder

6 eggs

¼ cup hazelnut liqueur

2 teaspoons almond extract

2 teaspoons vanilla

2 cups toasted hazelnuts, chopped*

1 cup white chocolate chips, melted (optional)

2 tablespoons very finely chopped hazelnuts (optional)

To toast nuts, spread in single layer on baking sheet. Bake in preheated 350°F oven 8 to 10 minutes or until golden brown, stirring frequently.

1. Preheat oven to 350°F. Line cookie sheets with parchment paper.

2. Combine flour, sugar and baking powder in medium bowl.

3. Beat eggs, liqueur, almond extract and vanilla in large bowl with electric mixer on high speed until frothy. Stir into flour mixture until well blended. Add nuts; knead gently four to five times until nuts are evenly distributed. Divide dough in half. Shape each half into 3-inch-wide flat loaves on prepared cookie sheets.

4. Bake 20 minutes until loaves are solid and sound hollow when tapped. Remove to wire racks; cool completely.

5. Cut in ¾-inch-thick slices. Place slices, cut side up, on prepared cookie sheets. Bake 15 minutes or until golden brown. Remove to wire racks; cool completely.

6. Dip one end of each cookie in melted white chocolate and sprinkle with finely chopped hazelnuts, if desired. Let stand on parchment paper until set.

Makes about 2 dozen biscotti

Finnish Spice Cookies (Nissu Nassu)

2 cups all-purpose flour

1½ teaspoons ground ginger

1½ teaspoons ground cinnamon

½ teaspoon ground cardamom

½ teaspoon ground cloves

⅔ cup packed brown sugar

½ cup (1 stick) butter, softened

½ teaspoon baking soda

3 to 5 tablespoons hot water

Royal Icing (recipe follows)

1. Combine flour, ginger, cinnamon, cardamom and cloves in medium bowl.

2. Beat brown sugar and butter in large bowl with electric mixer at medium-high speed until light and fluffy. Stir baking soda into 3 tablespoons hot water in small bowl until dissolved. Beat into butter mixture. Gradually add flour mixture at low speed until dough forms. (If dough is too crumbly, add additional hot water, 1 tablespoon at a time, until dough holds together.) Shape dough into two discs. Wrap separately in plastic wrap; refrigerate 30 minutes or until firm.

3. Preheat oven to 375°F. Line cookie sheets with parchment paper.

4. Working with one disc at a time, roll out dough on lightly floured surface to ⅛-inch thickness. Cut dough with floured 3-inch pig-shaped cookie cutter or desired cookie cutter. Place cutouts 1 inch apart on prepared cookie sheets. Gather scraps and reroll; cut additional cookies.

5. Bake 8 to 10 minutes or until firm and edges are lightly browned. Remove to wire racks; cool completely.

6. Prepare Royal Icing. Spoon icing into pastry bag fitted with writing tip. Decorate cooled cookies with icing. Let stand 1 hour or until set. Store tightly covered at room temperature or freeze up to 3 months.

Makes about 5 dozen cookies

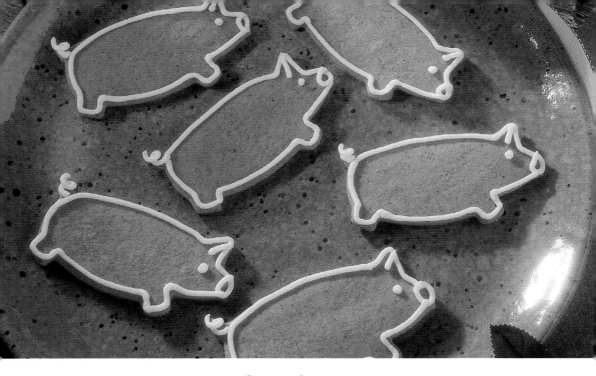

Royal Icing

1 egg white,* at room temperature

2 to 2¹/₂ cups sifted powdered sugar

¹/₂ teaspoon almond extract

Use only grade A clean, uncracked egg.

1. Beat egg white in small bowl at high speed of electric mixture until foamy.

2. Gradually add 2 cups powdered sugar and almond extract at low speed until moistened. Increase speed to high; beat until icing is stiff.

Spumone Bars

¾ cup (1½ sticks) butter, softened

⅔ cup sugar

3 egg yolks

1 teaspoon vanilla

¼ teaspoon baking powder

⅛ teaspoon salt

2 cups all-purpose flour

12 maraschino cherries, well drained and chopped

¼ cup chopped walnuts

¼ cup mint-flavored or plain semisweet chocolate chips

2 teaspoons water, divided

1. Preheat oven to 350°F. Beat butter and sugar in large bowl with electric mixer at medium-high speed until blended. Beat in egg yolks, vanilla, baking powder and salt until light and fluffy. Add flour at low speed until stiff dough forms.

2. Divide dough into three equal parts; place each part in separate small bowl. Add cherries and walnuts to one part; mix well. Melt chocolate chips in small saucepan over low heat, stirring constantly. Add melted chocolate and 1 teaspoon water to second part, mix well. Stir remaining 1 teaspoon water into third part. (If doughs are soft, refrigerate 10 minutes.)

3. Divide each color of dough into four equal pieces; roll each piece into 6-inch rope on lightly floured surface. Place one rope of each color side by side on ungreased cookie sheet. Flatten ropes so they attach together making one strip of three colors. With rolling pin, roll strip directly on cookie sheet until it measures 12×3 inches. With straight edge of knife, score strip crosswise at 1-inch intervals. Repeat with remaining ropes.

4. Bake 12 to 13 minutes or until set but not browned. While cookies are still warm, trim lengthwise edges to make them even and cut into individual cookies along score marks. Cool completely on cookie sheets.

Makes 4 dozen cookies

Danish Cookie Rings
(Vanillekranser)

½ cup blanched almonds

2 cups all-purpose flour

¾ cup sugar

¼ teaspoon baking powder

1 cup (2 sticks) butter, cut into small pieces

1 egg

1 tablespoon milk

1 tablespoon vanilla

15 candied red cherries

15 candied green cherries

1. Pulse almonds in food processor until finely ground, but not pasty. Place almonds, flour, sugar and baking powder in large bowl. Cut in butter with pastry blender or two knives until mixture is crumbly.

2. Beat egg, milk and vanilla in small bowl until well blended. Add egg mixture to flour mixture; stir until soft dough forms.

3. Line cookie sheets with parchment paper. Spoon dough into pastry bag fitted with medium star tip. Pipe 3-inch rings 2 inches apart on prepared cookie sheets. Refrigerate 15 minutes or until firm.

4. Preheat oven to 375°F. Cut red cherries into quarters. Cut green cherries into halves; cut each half into four slivers. Press red cherry quarter onto each ring where ends meet. Place green cherry sliver on either side of red cherry to form leaves.

5. Bake 8 to 10 minutes or until golden. Remove to wire racks; cool completely. Store tightly covered at room temperature or freeze up to 3 months.

Makes about 5 dozen cookies

Baklava

4 cups slivered almonds and/or walnuts (1 pound)

1¼ cups sugar, divided

2 teaspoons ground cinnamon

¼ teaspoon ground cloves

1 package (16 ounces) frozen phyllo dough (about 20 sheets), thawed

1 cup (2 sticks) butter, melted

1½ cups water

¾ cup honey

2 (2-inch-long) strips lemon peel

1 tablespoon fresh lemon juice

1 cinnamon stick

3 whole cloves

1. Place half of almonds in food processor. Pulse until nuts are finely chopped but not pasty. Place in medium bowl. Repeat with remaining nuts. Add ½ cup sugar, cinnamon and ground cloves to nuts; mix well.

2. Unroll phyllo dough; place on large sheet of waxed paper. Cut phyllo sheets in half crosswise to form two stacks, each about 13×9 inches. Cover phyllo with plastic wrap and damp, clean kitchen towel. (Phyllo dough dries out quickly if not covered.)

3. Preheat oven to 325°F. Brush 13×9-inch baking dish with some melted butter.

4. Place one phyllo sheet in bottom of dish, folding in edges if too long; brush surface with butter. Repeat with seven more phyllo sheets, brushing surface of each sheet with butter as they are layered. Sprinkle about ½ cup nut mixture evenly over layered phyllo.

5. Top nuts with three more layers of phyllo, brushing each sheet with butter. Sprinkle another ½ cup nut mixture on top. Repeat layering and brushing of three phyllo sheets with ½ cup nut mixture until there are a total of eight 3-sheet layers. Top final layer of nut mixture with remaining eight phyllo sheets, brushing each sheet with butter.

6. Cut baklava lengthwise into four equal sections, then cut diagonally at 1½-inch intervals to form diamond shapes. Sprinkle top lightly with water to prevent top phyllo layers from curling up during baking. Bake 50 to 60 minutes or until golden brown.

7. Meanwhile, combine 1½ cups water, remaining ¾ cup sugar, honey, lemon peel, lemon juice, cinnamon stick and whole cloves in medium saucepan. Bring to a boil over high heat. Reduce heat to low; simmer 15 minutes.

8. Strain hot syrup; drizzle evenly over hot baklava. Cool completely before serving.

Makes about 32 pieces

Santa's Favorite Cookies

Candy-Studded Wreaths

Easy All-Purpose Cookie Dough (page 60)

1 teaspoon vanilla

4 to 5 drops green food coloring

Mini red and green candy-coated chocolate pieces

1. Prepare dough, adding vanilla with egg. Divide dough in half; set one half aside. Add green color to remaining dough; beat until blended. Shape dough into discs. Wrap separately in plastic wrap; refrigerate 1 hour.

2. Preheat oven to 300°F. Shape green dough into 28 (5-inch) ropes. Repeat with plain dough. For each wreath, twist one green and one plain rope together, pressing ends together. Place on ungreased cookie sheets. Press candies onto wreaths.

3. Bake 15 to 18 minutes or until lightly browned. Cool on cookie sheets 5 minutes. Remove to wire racks; cool completely.

Makes about 2 dozen cookies

Eggnog Sandwich Cookies

COOKIES

- 2½ cups all-purpose flour
- ¼ teaspoon salt
- 1 cup (2 sticks) butter, softened
- 1¼ cups plus 1 tablespoon granulated sugar, divided
- 1 egg yolk
- ½ cup sour cream
- ½ teaspoon ground nutmeg
- ¼ teaspoon ground ginger

FILLING

- ½ cup (1 stick) butter, softened
- ¼ cup shortening
- 2½ cups powdered sugar
- 2 tablespoons brandy or milk

1. Preheat oven to 350°F. Line cookie sheets with parchment paper. Combine flour and salt in small bowl.

2. For cookies, beat 1 cup butter and 1¼ cups granulated sugar in large bowl with electric mixer at medium speed until light and fluffy. Add egg yolk; beat until blended. Add sour cream; beat until well blended. Gradually add flour mixture at low speed until well blended.

3. Shape teaspoonfuls of dough into balls. Place on prepared cookie sheets; flatten slightly. Combine remaining 1 tablespoon granulated sugar, nutmeg and ginger in small bowl; sprinkle over cookies.

4. Bake 12 minutes or until edges are golden. Cool on cookie sheets 5 minutes. Remove to wire racks; cool completely.

5. For filling, beat ½ cup butter and shortening in medium bowl until well blended. Add powdered sugar and brandy; beat until well blended. Spread or pipe filling on flat side of half of cookies. Top with remaining cookies, flat side down.

Makes about 6 dozen cookies

Frosted Butter Cookies

COOKIES

1½ cups (3 sticks) butter, softened

¾ cup granulated sugar

3 egg yolks

2 tablespoons orange juice

1 teaspoon vanilla

3 cups all-purpose flour

1 teaspoon baking powder

½ teaspoon salt

FROSTING

4 cups powdered sugar

½ cup (1 stick) butter, softened

3 to 4 tablespoons milk

2 teaspoons vanilla

Food coloring (optional)

Colored sugars, flaked coconut and cinnamon candies for decoration

1. For cookies, beat 1½ cups butter and granulated sugar in large bowl with electric mixer at medium-high speed until creamy. Add egg yolks; beat until light and fluffy. Beat in orange juice and vanilla. Gradually add flour, baking powder and salt at low speed until well mixed. Wrap dough in plastic wrap; refrigerate 2 to 3 hours or until firm.

2. Preheat oven to 350°F. Roll out dough, half at a time, to ¼-inch thickness on floured surface. Cut dough with desired cookie cutters. Place 1 inch apart on ungreased cookie sheets. Bake 6 to 10 minutes or until edges are lightly browned. Remove to wire racks; cool completely.

3. For frosting, beat powdered sugar, ½ cup butter, milk and vanilla in bowl until fluffy. If desired, divide frosting into small bowls and tint with food coloring. Frost cookies; decorate as desired.

Makes about 3 dozen cookies

TIP: If desired, decorate cookies with Royal Icing (page 155 or page 245) instead of the buttercream frosting.

Holiday Biscotti

2⅓ cups all-purpose flour
1½ teaspoons baking powder
¾ cup sugar
½ cup (1 stick) butter, softened
2 eggs

1 teaspoon vanilla
1½ cups dried cranberries
1 cup shelled pistachio nuts
(about 4¼ ounces)

1. Preheat oven to 375°F. Line cookie sheet with parchment paper. Combine flour and baking powder in medium bowl.

2. Beat sugar and butter in large bowl with electric mixer at medium speed until creamy. Beat in eggs and vanilla just until blended. Gradually add flour mixture, beating well at low speed after each addition. Stir in cranberries and pistachios.

3. Divide dough into thirds. Shape each piece into 9×2-inch log. (If dough is sticky, lightly dust hands with flour.) Place logs on prepared cookie sheet.

4. Bake 25 minutes or until tops are lightly browned (logs will be soft to the touch). Cool on cookie sheet until cool enough to handle. Cut logs diagonally into ½- to ¾-inch-thick slices using serrated knife.

5. *Reduce oven temperature to 325°F.* Place slices, cut side up, on cookie sheet (slices may touch). Bake 8 to 10 minutes or until edges are golden brown. Turn slices over; bake 8 to 10 minutes or until edges are golden brown. Remove to wire rack; cool completely. Store in airtight container.

Makes about 2 dozen biscotti

Chocolate Reindeer

1 cup granulated sugar
1 cup (2 sticks) butter, softened
1 egg
1 teaspoon vanilla
2 ounces semisweet chocolate, melted

2¼ cups all-purpose flour
1 teaspoon baking powder
¼ teaspoon salt
Royal Icing (page 155)
Assorted sprinkles and decors

1. Beat granulated sugar and butter in large bowl with electric mixer at high speed until fluffy. Beat in egg and vanilla. Add melted chocolate; beat until well blended. Add flour, baking powder and salt; beat until well blended. Divide dough in half. Shape each half into disc. Wrap separately in plastic wrap; refrigerate 2 hours or until firm.

2. Preheat oven to 325°F. Grease cookie sheets. Roll out dough on well-floured surface to ¼-inch thickness. Cut out shapes with 4-inch reindeer-shaped cookie cutter. Place cutouts 2 inches apart on prepared cookie sheets. Refrigerate 10 minutes.

3. Bake 13 to 15 minutes or until set. Cool completely on cookie sheets.

4. Prepare Royal Icing. Pipe icing onto reindeer; decorate as desired.

Makes about 2 dozen cookies

Sugar Cookies

2 cups all-purpose flour
$\frac{1}{2}$ teaspoon baking soda
$\frac{1}{8}$ teaspoon salt
$\frac{1}{2}$ cup (1 stick) butter
$\frac{1}{4}$ cup sugar

$\frac{1}{4}$ cup unsweetened applesauce
1 egg white
1 teaspoon vanilla
2 tablespoons red or green
 fine decorating sugar

1. Combine flour, baking soda and salt in medium bowl.

2. Beat butter and sugar in large bowl with electric mixer at medium speed 1 minute or until creamy. Add applesauce, egg white and vanilla. Beat at low speed just until blended; beat at medium speed until smooth.

3. Gradually add flour mixture to butter mixture, beating at low speed until well blended. Divide dough in half. Shape each half into 11-inch log. Wrap in plastic wrap; freeze at least 1 hour.

4. Preheat oven to 350°F. Cut logs crosswise into $\frac{1}{4}$-inch slices, turning log slightly after each slice. Dip half of one side of each cookie into decorating sugar. Place cookies, sugar side up, on cookie sheets.

5. Bake 6 to 8 minutes or until set. Cool on cookie sheets 2 minutes. Remove to wire racks; cool completely.

Makes about 6 dozen cookies

Rum Fruitcake Cookies

3 cups all-purpose flour
2 teaspoons baking powder
1 teaspoon baking soda
1 teaspoon salt
2 cups (8 ounces) chopped
    candied mixed fruit
1 cup nuts, coarsely chopped

1 cup raisins
1 cup sugar
3/4 cup shortening
3 eggs
1/3 cup orange juice
1 tablespoon rum extract

1. Preheat oven to 375°F. Line cookie sheets with parchment paper. Combine flour, baking powder, baking soda and salt in medium bowl. Add candied fruit, nuts and raisins.

2. Beat sugar and shortening in large bowl with electric mixer at medium speed until fluffy. Add eggs, orange juice and rum extract; beat 2 minutes. Stir flour mixture into shortening mixture. Drop dough by rounded teaspoonfuls 2 inches apart onto prepared cookie sheets.

3. Bake 10 to 12 minutes or until golden brown. Cool on cookie sheets 2 minutes. Remove to wire racks; cool completely.

Makes about 6 dozen cookies

Festive Candy Canes

1 cup powdered sugar

³/₄ cup (1¹/₂ sticks) butter, softened

1 egg

1 teaspoon peppermint extract

¹/₂ teaspoon vanilla

1²/₃ to 1³/₄ cups all-purpose flour

¹/₈ teaspoon salt

Red food coloring

1. Preheat oven to 350°F. Beat powdered sugar and butter in large bowl with electric mixer at medium speed until light and fluffy. Add egg, peppermint extract and vanilla; beat until well blended. Add flour and salt; beat until well blended. (Dough will be sticky.)

2. Divide dough in half. Tint half of dough with food coloring to desired shade of red. Leave remaining dough plain. For each candy cane, roll heaping teaspoonful red and plain dough into separate 5-inch ropes with floured hands. Twist ropes together; bend into candy cane shape. Place 2 inches apart on ungreased cookie sheets.

3. Bake 7 to 8 minutes or until set and edges are lightly browned. Cool on cookie sheets 2 minutes. Remove to wire racks; cool completely.

Makes about 2 dozen cookies

Chocolate-Dipped Cinnamon Thins

1¼ cups all-purpose flour

1½ teaspoons ground cinnamon

¼ teaspoon salt

1 cup (2 sticks) butter, softened

1 cup powdered sugar

1 egg

1 teaspoon vanilla

4 ounces bittersweet chocolate, melted

1. Combine flour, cinnamon and salt in small bowl. Beat butter in large bowl with electric mixer at medium speed until light and fluffy. Add powdered sugar; beat well. Add egg and vanilla. Gradually add flour mixture at low speed just until blended.

2. Place dough on sheet of waxed paper. Using waxed paper to hold dough, roll back and forth to form log about 2½ inches in diameter and 12 inches long. Wrap tightly in plastic wrap; refrigerate at least 2 hours or until firm. (Log may be frozen up to 3 months; thaw in refrigerator before baking.)

3. Preheat oven to 350°F. Cut dough into ¼-inch-thick slices. Place 2 inches apart on ungreased cookie sheets. Bake 10 minutes or until set. Cool on cookie sheets 2 minutes. Remove to wire racks; cool completely.

4. Dip each cookie into melted chocolate, coating 1 inch up sides. Transfer to wire racks or waxed paper; let stand at room temperature about 30 minutes or until chocolate is set. Store cookies between sheets of waxed paper at room temperature or in refrigerator.

Makes about 2 dozen cookies

Browned Butter Spritz Cookies

1½ cups (3 sticks) butter
2½ cups all-purpose flour
¼ cup cake flour
¼ teaspoon salt
½ cup granulated sugar
¼ cup powdered sugar

1 egg yolk
1 teaspoon vanilla
⅛ teaspoon almond extract
Decorating sugars, sprinkles and decors (optional)

1. Melt butter in medium heavy saucepan over medium heat until light amber, stirring frequently. Pour butter into large bowl. Cover and refrigerate 2 hours or until solid.

2. Preheat oven to 350°F. Let browned butter stand at room temperature 15 minutes. Combine all-purpose flour, cake flour and salt in small bowl.

3. Beat browned butter, granulated sugar and powdered sugar in large bowl with electric mixer at medium speed until light and fluffy. Add egg yolk, vanilla and almond extract; beat until well blended. Add flour mixture; beat until well blended.

4. Fit cookie press with desired plate. Fill press with dough; press dough 1 inch apart on ungreased cookie sheets. If desired, change plates for different shapes after each batch.

5. Bake 10 minutes or until lightly browned. Cool on cookie sheets 5 minutes. Remove to wire racks; cool completely. Decorate as desired.

Makes about 8 dozen cookies

TIP: To add even more holiday sparkle to these delicious cookies, press red or green glacé cherry halves into the centers before baking. For pretty trees or wreaths, tint the dough with green food coloring before pressing.

Buttery Almond Cutouts

1½ cups granulated sugar

1 cup (2 sticks) butter, softened

¾ cup sour cream

2 eggs

3 teaspoons almond extract, divided

1 teaspoon vanilla

4⅓ cups all-purpose flour

1 teaspoon baking powder

1 teaspoon baking soda

½ teaspoon salt

2 cups powdered sugar

2 tablespoons milk

1 tablespoon light corn syrup

Assorted food coloring, decorating gels, decorating sugars, sprinkles and decors

1. Beat granulated sugar and butter in large bowl with electric mixer at medium speed until light and fluffy. Add sour cream, eggs, 2 teaspoons almond extract and vanilla; beat until smooth. Add flour, baking powder, baking soda and salt; beat until well blended. Divide dough into four pieces; shape each piece into disc. Wrap each disc tightly with plastic wrap. Refrigerate at least 3 hours or up to 3 days.

2. For icing, combine powdered sugar, milk, corn syrup and remaining 1 teaspoon almond extract in small bowl; stir until smooth. Cover and refrigerate until ready to use or up to 3 days.

3. Preheat oven to 375°F. Roll out dough on floured surface to ¼-inch thickness. Cut out shapes using 2½-inch cookie cutters. Place cutouts 2 inches apart on ungreased cookie sheets. Bake 7 to 8 minutes or until edges are set and lightly browned. Remove to wire racks; cool completely.

4. Tint icing with desired food coloring. Frost and decorate cookies as desired; let stand until set.

Makes about 3 dozen cookies

NOTE: To freeze dough, place wrapped discs in resealable plastic food storage bags. Thaw at room temperature before using. Or cut out dough, bake and cool cookies completely. Freeze unglazed cookies for up to 2 months. Thaw and glaze as desired.

Chocolate-Cherry Slice 'n' Bake Cookies

³/₄ cup (1¹/₂ sticks) butter or margarine, softened

1 cup sugar

1 egg

1¹/₂ teaspoons vanilla extract

2¹/₄ cups all-purpose flour

2 teaspoons baking powder

¹/₂ teaspoon salt

¹/₄ cup finely chopped maraschino cherries

¹/₂ teaspoon almond extract

Red food color

¹/₃ cup HERSHEY'S® Cocoa

¹/₄ teaspoon baking soda

4 teaspoons water

COCOA ALMOND GLAZE (recipe follows, optional)

1. Beat butter, sugar, egg and vanilla in large bowl until fluffy. Stir together flour, baking powder and salt; gradually add to butter mixture, beating until mixture forms a smooth dough. Remove 1¹/₄ cups dough to medium bowl; blend in cherries, almond extract and about 6 drops food color.

2. Stir together cocoa and baking soda. Add with water to remaining dough; blend until smooth. Divide chocolate dough in half; roll each half between two sheets of wax paper, forming 12×4¹/₂-inch rectangle. Remove top sheet of wax paper. Divide cherry mixture in half; with floured hands, shape each half into 12-inch roll. Place one roll in center of each rectangle; wrap chocolate dough around roll, forming one large roll. Wrap each roll in plastic wrap. Refrigerate about 6 hours or until firm.

3. Heat oven to 350°F.

4. Cut rolls into ¹/₄-inch-thick slices; place on ungreased cookie sheet. Bake 7 minutes or until set. Cool 1 minute; remove from cookie sheet to wire rack. Cool completely. Decorate cookies with COCOA ALMOND GLAZE, if desired.

Makes about 7¹/₂ dozen cookies

Cocoa Almond Glaze

2 tablespoons butter or margarine
2 tablespoons HERSHEY'S® Cocoa

2 tablespoons water
1 cup powdered sugar
⅛ teaspoon almond extract

Melt butter in small saucepan over low heat. Add cocoa and water; stir constantly until mixture thickens. Do not boil. Remove from heat. Add powdered sugar and almond extract, beating until smooth and of desired consistency. Add additional water, ½ teaspoon at a time, if needed.

Makes about ½ cup glaze

Brandy Snaps
with Lemon Ricotta Cream

³/₄ cup sugar, divided
**1 cup (2 sticks) butter,
softened, divided**
¹/₃ cup light corn syrup
1 cup all-purpose flour

1 tablespoon brandy or cognac
¹/₂ cup ricotta cheese
1 tablespoon lemon juice
2 teaspoons grated lemon peel

1. Preheat oven to 325°F. Combine ¹/₂ cup sugar, ¹/₂ cup butter and corn syrup in medium saucepan. Cook and stir over medium heat until butter is melted. Stir in flour and brandy.

2. Drop batter by level tablespoonfuls about 3 inches apart onto ungreased cookie sheets, spacing to fit four cookies per sheet. Bake one cookie sheet at a time 12 minutes or until golden brown.

3. Cool on cookie sheets 1 minute. Remove each cookie and quickly wrap around wooden spoon handle.

4. For filling, combine remaining ¹/₂ cup butter, ricotta, remaining ¹/₄ cup sugar, lemon juice and lemon peel in food processor; process until smooth.

5. Spoon filling into pastry bag fitted with plain or star tip. Fill cookies just before serving.

Makes 2 dozen cookies

Snowpeople Cookies

2¼ cups all-purpose flour

½ teaspoon baking soda

1 package (8 ounces) cream cheese, softened

1 cup powdered sugar

½ cup (1 stick) butter, softened

½ teaspoon almond extract

Additional sifted powdered sugar

12 sticks red or striped chewing gum

Mini candy-coated chocolate pieces

Red gummy candies, flattened and trimmed

Decorating icing

1. Preheat oven to 325°F. Line cookies sheets with parchment paper. Combine flour and baking soda in medium bowl.

2. Beat cream cheese, 1 cup powdered sugar, butter and almond extract in large bowl with electric mixer at medium speed until well blended.

3. Shape dough into equal number of ½-inch, 1-inch and 1½-inch diameter balls. Using one small, medium and large ball per snowperson, place balls, nearly touching, on prepared cookie sheets. Flatten each ball to ¼-inch thickness using bottom of glass dipped in flour.

4. Bake about 15 minutes or until edges are lightly browned. Cool on cookie sheets 1 minute. Remove to wire racks; cool completely.

5. Sprinkle each snowperson with additional sifted powdered sugar. Using one stick of gum, make scarf with fringed ends for each snowperson. Use chocolate pieces for eyes and gummy candies for mouths, securing with decorating icing.

Makes 1 dozen snowpeople

Double Chocolate Sandwich Cookies

1 package (about 16 ounces) refrigerated sugar cookie dough

1 bar (3½ to 4 ounces) bittersweet chocolate, chopped

2 teaspoons butter

¾ cup milk chocolate chips

1. Preheat oven to 350°F. Remove dough from wrapper, retaining log shape.

2. Cut dough into ¼-inch-thick slices; place 2 inches apart on ungreased cookie sheets. Cut centers out of half of cookies using ½-inch round cookie cutter.

3. Bake 10 to 12 minutes or until edges are lightly browned. Cool on cookie sheets 2 minutes. Remove to wire racks; cool completely.

4. Heat bittersweet chocolate and butter in small heavy saucepan over low heat, stirring frequently, until chocolate is melted. Spread chocolate over flat sides of cookies without holes; immediately top with cutout cookies.

5. Place milk chocolate chips in resealable food storage bag; seal bag. Microwave on MEDIUM (50%) 1½ minutes. Turn bag over; microwave 1 to 1½ minutes more or chocolate is until melted. Knead bag until chocolate is smooth.

6. Cut tiny corner off bag; drizzle chocolate decoratively over sandwich cookies. Let stand 30 minutes or until chocolate is set.

Makes about 1½ dozen cookies

Gingerbread People

½ cup (1 stick) butter, softened
½ cup packed brown sugar
⅓ cup water
⅓ cup molasses
1 egg
4 cups all-purpose flour
2 teaspoons baking soda

1 teaspoon ground ginger
½ teaspoon ground allspice
½ teaspoon ground cinnamon
½ teaspoon ground cloves
Royal Icing (page 155)
Assorted candies

1. Beat butter and brown sugar in large bowl with electric mixer at medium speed until creamy. Add water, molasses and egg; beat until blended. Add flour, baking soda, ginger, allspice, cinnamon and cloves; beat until well blended. Shape dough into disc; wrap tightly with plastic wrap. Refrigerate 2 hours or until firm.

2. Preheat oven to 350°F. Line cookie sheets. with parchment paper Roll out dough on lightly floured surface with lightly floured rolling pin to ⅛-inch thickness. Cut out shapes with cookie cutters. Place cutouts 2 inches apart on prepared cookie sheets.

3. Bake 12 to 15 minutes or until set. Cool on cookie sheets 1 minute. Remove to wire racks; cool completely.

4. Prepare Royal Icing. Decorate cookies with icing and candies. Store in airtight containers.

Makes about 4½ dozen cookies

Holiday
Triple Chocolate Yule Logs

1³/₄ cups all-purpose flour
³/₄ cup powdered sugar
¹/₄ cup unsweetened cocoa
    powder
¹/₈ teaspoon salt

1 cup (2 sticks) butter,
    softened
1 teaspoon vanilla
1 cup white chocolate chips
    Chocolate sprinkles

1. Combine flour, powdered sugar, cocoa and salt in medium bowl. Beat butter and vanilla in large bowl with electric mixer at medium speed until fluffy. Gradually beat in flour mixture until well blended. Wrap dough in plastic wrap; refrigerate 30 minutes or until firm.

2. Preheat oven to 350°F. Shape dough into 2-inch logs about ¹/₂ inch thick. Place 2 inches apart on ungreased cookie sheets.

3. Bake 12 minutes or until set. Cool on cookie sheets 2 minutes. Remove to wire racks; cool completely.

4. Place white chocolate chips in small microwavable bowl. Microwave on HIGH 45 seconds; stir until completely melted. Place chocolate sprinkles in another small bowl. Dip both ends of cookies into melted white chocolate, then into chocolate sprinkles. Place on wire racks. Let stand 30 minutes or until set.

Makes about 3 dozen cookies

Chocolate Pinwheels

2 cups (4 sticks) butter, softened

1 cup powdered sugar

1/4 cup packed brown sugar

1/2 teaspoon salt

4 cups all-purpose flour

1/2 cup semisweet chocolate chips, melted

1 tablespoon unsweetened cocoa powder

1. Beat butter, powdered sugar, brown sugar and salt in large bowl with electric mixer at medium speed 2 minutes or until light and fluffy. Gradually add flour at low speed until well blended. Divide dough in half; set one half aside. Add melted chocolate and cocoa to remaining dough; beat until well blended.

2. Shape the chocolate and plain doughs each into four portions. Roll one plain portion into 12×6-inch rectangle on lightly floured surface; transfer to sheet of parchment paper or plastic wrap. Roll one portion of chocolate dough into 12×6-inch rectangle on lightly floured surface; place over plain dough. Tightly roll up from one long end to form 12-inch log. If dough crumbles or breaks, press back together and continue to roll (the effect will be marbled, not spiraled, but just as attractive). Wrap in plastic wrap; refrigerate 1 hour. Repeat with remaining dough.

3. Preheat oven to 300°F. Cut each log into 20 slices; place on ungreased cookie sheets. Bake 13 to 15 minutes or until cookies are set and lightly browned. Cool on cookie sheets 5 minutes. Remove to wire racks; cool completely.

Makes about 6 dozen cookies

Year-Round Treats

Pots of Gold

1 package (about 16 ounces) refrigerated sugar cookie dough

¼ cup unsweetened cocoa powder

Royal Icing (page 155)

Green and black food coloring

Yellow mini candy-coated chocolate pieces

1. Preheat oven to 350°F. Remove dough from wrapper; place in large bowl. Add cocoa; beat until well blended.

2. Roll out dough on lightly floured surface to ⅛-inch thickness. Cut out pots with 4-inch cookie cutter. (Halloween cauldron cookie cutter may be used.)

3. Place cookies 2 inches apart on ungreased cookie sheets. Bake about 6 minutes or until firm. Cool on cookie sheets 2 minutes. Remove to wire racks; cool completely.

4. Prepare Royal Icing. Spoon two thirds of icing into small bowl; tint with green food coloring. Spoon remaining one third of icing into small bowl; tint with black food coloring. Frost bottom of pots in green; frost top of pots in black. Arrange yellow candies over black frosting to resemble gold.

Makes about 2½ dozen cookies

Irish Flag Cookies

1½ cups all-purpose flour
1 teaspoon baking powder
½ teaspoon salt
¾ cup granulated sugar
¾ cup packed brown sugar
½ cup (1 stick) butter, softened
2 eggs

2 teaspoons vanilla
1 package (12 ounces)
  semisweet chocolate chips
Prepared white frosting
Green and orange food
  coloring and decorating gels

1. Preheat oven to 350°F. Spray 13×9-inch baking pan with nonstick cooking spray. Combine flour, baking powder and salt in small bowl.

2. Beat granulated sugar, brown sugar and butter in large bowl with electric mixer at medium speed until light and fluffy. Beat in eggs and vanilla. Add flour mixture; beat at low speed until well blended. Stir in chocolate chips. Spread batter evenly in prepared pan.

3. Bake 25 to 30 minutes or until golden brown. Cool completely in pan on wire rack. Cut into 3¼×1½-inch bars.

4. Divide frosting among three small bowls. Tint one with green food coloring and one with orange food coloring; leave remaining frosting white. Frost cookies in stripes to resemble Irish flag.

Makes 2 dozen cookies

Fluffy Cottontails

¾ cup sugar
½ cup (1 stick) butter, softened
½ cup shortening
1 teaspoon vanilla
2 cups all-purpose flour
⅔ cup malted milk powder

¼ teaspoon salt
Malted milk balls
Royal Icing (page 155)
Assorted food coloring
Mini marshmallows

1. Preheat oven to 350°F. Line cookie sheets with parchment paper. Beat sugar, butter, shortening and vanilla in large bowl with electric mixer at medium speed. Add flour, malted milk powder and salt at low speed until well blended.

2. For bunny bodies, shape heaping teaspoonfuls of dough around malted milk balls. For bunny heads, shape scant teaspoonfuls of dough into balls. For each bunny, press body and head together and place 2 inches apart on prepared cookie sheets. Shape ½ teaspoon of dough into 2 ears; press gently into head.

3. Bake 8 minutes or until lightly browned. Cool on cookie sheets 1 minute. Remove to wire racks; cool completely.

4. Prepare Royal Icing; tint desired colors. Decorate cookies with icing. Cut marshmallows in half; immediately place marshmallow halves on cookies to resemble bunny tails. Let stand 5 minutes or until set.

Makes 2½ dozen cookies

Mini Wedding Cakes

1½ cups all-purpose flour
1 teaspoon baking powder
½ teaspoon salt
½ cup (1 stick) butter, softened
¾ cup granulated sugar
¾ cup packed brown sugar

2 eggs
2 teaspoons vanilla
White Glaze (recipe follows)
Royal Icing (page 155)
Assorted colored decors

1. Preheat oven to 350°F. Spray 15×10-inch jelly-roll pan with nonstick cooking spray. Combine flour, baking powder and salt in small bowl.

2. Beat butter, granulated sugar and brown sugar in large bowl with electric mixer at medium-high speed until fluffy. Beat in eggs and vanilla. Add flour mixture at low speed until well blended. Spread batter evenly in prepared pan. Bake 15 to 20 minutes or until golden brown. Remove pan to wire rack; cool completely.

3. Using 2¾-inch, 2-inch and ¾-inch round cutters, cut same number of circles for each size. Prepare White Glaze. Spread some of glaze on tops of large and medium circles. Place medium circles on large circles; place small circles on medium circles. Let stand until glaze is set.

4. Prepare Royal Icing. Place cookies on wire racks set over waxed paper. Spread glaze over cookies to cover. Decorate as desired with Royal Icing and decors. Let stand until icing is set.

Makes about 10 large cookies

WHITE GLAZE: Combine 4 cups powdered sugar, 6 tablespoons water and 3 tablespoons meringue powder in large bowl. Beat with electric mixer at high speed 6 to 7 minutes to make a medium-thick pourable glaze. (Meringue powder is a dried egg white-based powder. It can be found in the cake decorating section of most craft stores.)

Wedding Bells

1 cup (2 sticks) butter,
   softened
³/₄ cup granulated sugar
2 eggs
2½ cups all-purpose flour
1 teaspoon baking powder

¼ teaspoon salt
¼ teaspoon ground cinnamon
Royal Icing (page 155)
Assorted food coloring
Colored sprinkles, sugars
   and decors

1. Beat butter and granulated sugar in large bowl with electric mixer at medium speed until creamy. Add eggs; beat until fluffy. Stir in flour, baking powder, salt and cinnamon at low speed until well blended. Shape dough into two discs. Wrap separately in plastic wrap; refrigerate 2 hours or until firm.

2. Preheat oven to 350°F. Line cookie sheets with parchment paper. Roll out dough between sheets of parchment paper to ¼-inch thickness. Cut out bells with 2½-inch cookie cutter. Place 1 inch apart on prepared cookie sheets. Make small hole in top of each bell with drinking straw or skewer.

3. Bake 10 to 12 minutes or until edges are lightly browned. Cool on cookie sheets 1 minute. Remove to wire racks; cool completely.

4. Prepare Royal Icing; tint desired colors. Decorate cookies with icings, sprinkles, sugars and decors. Tie two bells together with ribbon.

Makes 3 dozen cookies

Yummy Rattles

1½ cups (3 sticks) butter,
  softened
1 cup packed brown sugar
2 egg yolks
3½ cups all-purpose flour
1½ teaspoons baking powder

¼ teaspoon salt
Royal Icing (page 155)
Assorted food coloring
Assorted small candies and
  decors

1. Combine butter, brown sugar and egg yolks in medium bowl. Add flour, baking powder and salt; mix well. Shape dough into two discs. Wrap separately in plastic wrap; refrigerate 2 hours or until firm.

2. Preheat oven to 350°F. Line cookie sheets with parchment paper. Roll out dough between sheets of parchment paper to ¼-inch thickness. Cut out 24 large circles with 2½-inch round cookie cutter and 24 small circles with 1-inch round cookie cutter. Shape remaining dough into 24 (2½-inch) logs.

3. To make rattles, place large circles on prepared cookie sheets. Press one log at side of each large circle; press small circle at opposite end of each log. Flatten logs slightly.

4. Bake 8 to 10 minutes or until edges are lightly browned. Cool on cookie sheets 2 minutes. Remove to wire racks; cool completely.

5. Prepare Royal Icing; tint desired colors. Decorate cookies with icing, small candies and decors as desired.

Makes 2 dozen cookies

High-Flying Flags

3/4 cup (1 1/2 sticks) butter, softened
1/4 cup granulated sugar
1/4 cup packed brown sugar
1 egg yolk
1 3/4 cups all-purpose flour
3/4 teaspoon baking powder

1/8 teaspoon salt
Lollipop sticks
Royal Icing (page 155)
White sugar stars and red string licorice

1. Beat butter, granulated sugar, brown sugar and egg yolk in large bowl with electric mixer at medium speed until creamy. Add flour, baking powder and salt at low speed until well blended. Wrap dough in plastic wrap; refrigerate 1 hour or until firm.

2. Preheat oven to 350°F. Line cookie sheets with parchment paper. Roll out dough on lightly floured surface to 1/4-inch thickness. Cut out dough using 3-inch flag-shaped cookie cutter. Place lollipop stick under left side of each flag; press gently to adhere. Place flags 2 inches apart on prepared cookie sheets.

3. Bake 8 to 10 minutes or until edges are lightly browned. Cool on cookie sheets 2 minutes. Remove to wire racks; cool completely.

4. Prepare Royal Icing; tint half blue and leave half white. Spread blue icing in square in upper left corner of each flag; arrange sugar stars on blue icing. Spread white icing over plain sections of cookies. Place strips of red licorice on white icing; let set.

Makes 3 dozen cookies

Spiced Autumn Leaves

1½ cups (3 sticks) butter, softened

¾ cup packed brown sugar

½ teaspoon vanilla

3½ cups all-purpose flour

1 teaspoon ground cinnamon

½ teaspoon salt

⅛ teaspoon ground ginger

⅛ teaspoon ground cloves

2 tablespoons unsweetened cocoa powder

Yellow, orange and red food coloring

⅓ cup semisweet chocolate chips

1. Beat butter, brown sugar and vanilla in large bowl with electric mixer at medium speed until light and fluffy. Add flour, cinnamon, salt, ginger and cloves at low speed until well blended.

2. Divide dough into five equal portions; place in separate small bowls. Stir cocoa into one portion until well blended. (If dough is too dry and will not hold together, add 1 teaspoon water; beat until well blended and dough forms a ball.) Add yellow food coloring, drop by drop, to one portion; stir until well blended and desired color is reached. Repeat with two portions and orange and red food colorings. Leave remaining one portion plain.

3. Preheat oven to 350°F. Line cookie sheets with parchment paper. Working with half of each dough portion, press colors together lightly. Roll out dough on lightly floured surface to ¼-inch thickness. Cut dough with leaf-shaped cookie cutters. Place 2 inches apart on prepared cookie sheets. Repeat with remaining dough and scraps.

4. Bake 10 to 15 minutes or until edges are lightly browned. Cool on cookie sheets 2 minutes. Remove to wire racks; cool completely.

5. Place chocolate chips in small resealable food storage bag; seal. Microwave on HIGH 30 seconds; knead bag lightly. Microwave on HIGH at 15-second intervals until smooth and melted, kneading bag after each interval. Cut off tiny corner of bag. Pipe chocolate onto cookies in vein patterns.

Makes about 2 dozen cookies

Brrrrownie Cats

1 cup (2 sticks) butter

4 ounces unsweetened chocolate

1½ cups sugar

3 eggs

1 cup all-purpose flour

¼ teaspoon salt

Black frosting, sprinkles and decors

1. Preheat oven to 350°F. Spray 13×9-inch baking pan with nonstick cooking spray. Melt butter and chocolate in top of double boiler, stirring occasionally.*

2. Transfer butter mixture to large bowl. Stir in sugar until well blended. Beat in eggs, one at a time. Stir in flour and salt. Spread batter into prepared pan.

3. Bake 20 to 25 minutes or just until firm. Cool completely on wire rack.

4. Cut brownies into cat shapes using Halloween cookie cutters. Decorate as desired.

Or place unwrapped chocolate squares in small microwavable bowl. Microwave on HIGH 1 to 1½ minutes, stirring after 1 minute.

Makes about 2 dozen brownies

Peanut Butter Pumpkins

1 package (about 16 ounces)
refrigerated peanut
butter cookie dough
½ cup all-purpose flour
3 cups powdered sugar, sifted

4 to 5 tablespoons milk
Orange food coloring
Orange decorating sugar
Pretzel sticks
Green chewy fruit candies

1. Let dough stand at room temperature 15 minutes. Line cookie sheets with parchment paper.

2. Combine dough and flour in medium bowl until well blended. Shape tablespoonfuls of dough into balls; place on prepared cookie sheets. Freeze 20 minutes or until firm.

3. Press side of toothpick (not tip) into dough balls from top to bottom to create grooves in pumpkins. Press toothpick into top of each pumpkin to create hole for stem. Freeze 15 minutes. Preheat oven to 350°F.

4. Bake 12 minutes or until lightly browned. Immediately press toothpick into tops of pumpkins again for stem. Cool on cookie sheets 5 minutes. Remove to wire racks; cool completely.

5. Place wire racks over sheets of waxed paper. Place powdered sugar in medium bowl; whisk in milk until blended. (Glaze should be thick but pourable.) Stir in food coloring until desired shade of orange is reached.

6. Holding bottoms of cookies, dip tops of cookies into glaze, turning to coat. Let excess glaze drip off before placing cookies, right side up, on wire racks. Sprinkle with decorating sugar. Break pretzel sticks into ½-inch pieces; insert into center holes for stems.

7. Press candies with palm of hand to flatten. (Candies can also be stretched with fingers.) Cut out small (¼-inch) leaf shapes with scissors. Arrange leaves around pretzel stems.

Makes about 2 dozen pumpkins

Sugar and Spice Halloween Cookies

2¹⁄₃ cups all-purpose flour

2 teaspoons ground cinnamon

1¹⁄₂ teaspoons baking powder

1¹⁄₂ teaspoons ground ginger

¹⁄₂ teaspoon salt

¹⁄₄ teaspoon ground nutmeg

³⁄₄ cup (1¹⁄₂ sticks) butter, softened

¹⁄₂ cup packed brown sugar

¹⁄₂ cup molasses

1 egg

Royal Icing (page 155)

Sparkling sugars

1. Combine flour, cinnamon, baking powder, ginger, salt and nutmeg in medium bowl. Beat butter and brown sugar in large bowl with electric mixer at medium speed until light and fluffy. Add molasses and egg; beat until well blended. Gradually beat in flour mixture just until combined.

2. Shape dough into two balls; press into 2-inch-thick discs. Wrap in plastic wrap; refrigerate at least 1 hour or until firm. (Dough may be prepared up to 2 days before baking.) Let stand at room temperature to soften slightly before rolling out.

3. Preheat oven to 350°F. Roll out dough on lightly floured surface to ¹⁄₄-inch thickness. Cut out shapes with Halloween cookie cutters. Place cutouts on ungreased cookie sheets.

4. Bake 12 to 14 minutes or until centers of cookies are firm to the touch. Cool on cookie sheets 1 minute. Remove to wire racks; cool completely.

5. Prepare Royal Icing; tint desired colors. Frost cookies and decorate as desired.

Makes 2 to 3 dozen cookies

Tom Turkeys

1 cup (2 sticks) butter, softened

½ cup powdered sugar

2 tablespoons packed brown sugar

¼ teaspoon salt

1 egg

2 cups all-purpose flour

¾ cup chocolate frosting

¼ to ½ cup white frosting

Red gummy candies

Mini semisweet chocolate chips

Red candy-coated sunflower seeds

Black string licorice

Red, orange and yellow candy-coated chocolate pieces

1. Beat butter, powdered sugar, brown sugar and salt in large bowl with electric mixer at medium speed 2 minutes or until light and fluffy. Add egg; beat until well blended. Add flour, ½ cup at a time, beating well after each addition.

2. Shape dough into disc; wrap tightly in plastic wrap. Refrigerate at least 1 hour or until firm.

3. Preheat oven to 300°F. Roll out dough on lightly floured surface to ⅛-inch thickness. Cut out turkeys using 2½- to 3-inch cookie cutter. Place cutouts 1 inch apart on ungreased cookie sheets.

4. Bake 20 to 25 minutes or until edges are light golden brown. Cool on cookie sheets 1 minute. Remove to wire racks; cool completely.

5. Combine chocolate frosting and ¼ cup white frosting in medium bowl until well blended; add additional white frosting for lighter color. Spread frosting over cookies.

6. Press red gummy candies with palm of hand to flatten; cut out small triangles for beaks. Arrange mini chocolate chips, candy-coated sunflower seeds and red candy triangles on cookies to create turkey faces. Cut ¼-inch lengths from licorice; place on turkey feet. Decorate body of turkeys with candy-coated chocolate pieces.

Makes about 12 cookies

Autumn Pumpkin Bars

2 cups all-purpose flour

2 teaspoons pumpkin pie spice

1 teaspoon baking powder

1/2 teaspoon salt

1/4 teaspoon baking soda

1 cup plus 2 tablespoons packed brown sugar

3/4 cup (1 1/2 sticks) butter, softened

1 egg

1 1/2 cups solid-pack pumpkin

1 teaspoon vanilla

1 cup semisweet chocolate chips, melted

1. Preheat oven to 350°F. Spray 13×9-inch baking pan with nonstick cooking spray. Whisk flour, pumpkin pie spice, baking powder, salt and baking soda in medium bowl.

2. Beat brown sugar and butter in large bowl with electric mixer at medium speed 3 minutes or until well blended. Beat in egg until blended. Beat in pumpkin and vanilla. (Mixture may look curdled.) Gradually add flour mixture, beating at low speed just until blended. Spread batter evenly in prepared pan.

3. Bake 25 minutes or until toothpick inserted into center comes out clean. Cool completely in pan on wire rack.

4. Cut out pumpkin and leaf shapes with 2- to 3-inch cookie cutters. Place melted chocolate in pastry bag or small resealable food storage bag with small corner cut off. Pipe veins on leaves and lines on pumpkins with chocolate.

Makes about 1 1/2 dozen bars

Hanukkah Cookies

½ cup (1 stick) butter, softened
½ cup sugar
3 ounces cream cheese
¼ cup honey
1 egg
½ teaspoon vanilla

2½ cups all-purpose flour
⅓ cup finely ground walnuts
1 teaspoon baking powder
¼ teaspoon salt
Royal Icing (page 155)
Gel paste food coloring

1. Beat butter, sugar, cream cheese, honey, egg and vanilla in large bowl with electric mixer at medium speed until creamy. Stir in flour, walnuts, baking powder and salt at low speed until well blended. Shape dough into disc. Wrap in plastic wrap; refrigerate about 2 hours or until firm.

2. Preheat oven to 350°F. Line cookie sheets with parchment paper. Roll out dough to ¼-inch thickness on floured surface with lightly floured rolling pin. Cut out dough with 2½-inch dreidel and 6-pointed star cookie cutters. Place 2 inches apart on prepared cookie sheets.

3. Bake 8 to 10 minutes or until edges are lightly browned. Cool on cookie sheets 2 minutes. Remove to wire racks; cool completely.

4. Prepare Royal Icing; tint desired colors, leaving some icing white. Decorate cookies with icing.

Makes 3½ dozen cookies

Anytime Delights

Wiggly Worms

Easy All-Purpose Cookie
Dough (page 60)

1½ teaspoons ground cinnamon

Small tube white frosting

Colored sprinkles and/or
small candies (optional)

1. Prepare cookie dough as directed, stirring in cinnamon with flour. Wrap dough in plastic wrap; refrigerate 1 hour.

2. Preheat oven to 300°F. For each worm, roll 1½ tablespoons dough between palms until about 6 inches long and ½ inch thick. Place on ungreased cookie sheets, curving dough into squiggly worm shapes. Refrigerate at least 15 minutes before baking.

3. Bake 17 to 19 minutes or until edges are light golden brown. Cool on cookie sheets 1 minute. Remove to wire racks; cool completely.

4. Decorate worms with frosting and sprinkles as desired.

Makes about 2½ dozen cookies

Butter Pretzel Cookies

3/4 cup (1 1/2 sticks) butter, softened
1/4 cup granulated sugar
1/4 cup packed brown sugar
1 egg yolk

1 3/4 cups all-purpose flour
3/4 teaspoon baking powder
1/8 teaspoon salt
Coarse sugar

1. Combine butter, granulated sugar, brown sugar and egg yolk in medium bowl. Add flour, baking powder and salt; mix well.

2. Cover; refrigerate about 4 hours or until firm.

3. Preheat oven to 350°F. Line cookie sheets with parchment paper.

4. Divide dough into four equal portions. Reserve one portion; refrigerate remaining three portions. Divide reserved dough into four equal pieces. Shape each dough piece on lightly floured surface to 12-inch rope; sprinkle with coarse sugar.

5. Shape each rope into pretzel shape; place on prepared cookie sheets. Repeat with remaining dough pieces.

6. Bake 14 to 18 minutes or until edges begin to brown. Cool cookies on cookie sheets 1 minute. Remove to wire racks; cool completely.

Makes 16 cookies

Letters of the Alphabet

1½ cups all-purpose flour

1 teaspoon ground cinnamon

½ teaspoon baking soda

½ teaspoon salt

½ teaspoon ground ginger

¼ teaspoon baking powder

½ cup shortening

⅓ cup packed brown sugar

¼ cup dark molasses

1 egg white

½ teaspoon vanilla

Royal Icing (page 155)

Colored sugars, sprinkles and assorted small candies

1. Combine flour, cinnamon, baking soda, salt, ginger and baking powder in small bowl.

2. Beat shortening, brown sugar, molasses, egg white and vanilla in large bowl at high speed of electric mixer until smooth. Add flour mixture at low speed. Shape dough into four discs. Wrap separately in plastic wrap; refrigerate 2 hours or until firm.

3. Preheat oven to 350°F. Line cookie sheets with parchment paper.

4. Roll out dough on well-floured surface to ⅛-inch thickness. Sprinkle with flour to minimize sticking, if necessary. Cut out letters using 2½-inch cookie cutters; place on prepared cookie sheets.

5. Bake 6 to 8 minutes or until firm and edges begin to brown. Remove to wire racks; cool completely.

6. Prepare Royal Icing; tint desired colors. Decorate cookies with icing, colored sugars, sprinkles and assorted small candies.

Makes about 5 dozen cookies

Panda Pals

3½ cups all-purpose flour
1 teaspoon salt
1½ cups sugar
1 cup (2 sticks) butter, softened
2 eggs

1 teaspoon almond extract
1 teaspoon vanilla
1 cup prepared white or vanilla frosting
Black gel food coloring
Black jelly beans, cut in half

1. Combine flour and salt in medium bowl.

2. Beat sugar and butter in large bowl with electric mixer at medium speed until light and fluffy. Add eggs, one at a time, beating until blended after each addition. Add almond extract and vanilla; beat until blended. Gradually add flour mixture at low speed, beating until well blended. Shape dough into two discs. Wrap separately in plastic wrap; refrigerate 1 hour or until firm.

3. Preheat oven to 350°F. Line cookie sheets with parchment paper. Roll out dough on lightly floured surface to ¼-inch thickness. Cut out 12 large circles with 3-inch round cookie cutter, 12 medium circles with 1¾-inch round cookie cutter and 24 small circles with 1¼-inch round cookie cutter.

4. Place large circles 3 inches apart on prepared cookie sheets. Place two small circles next to each large circle for ears. Place medium circles 1 inch apart on separate prepared cookie sheet. Refrigerate 15 minutes.

5. Bake large circles 15 to 17 minutes or until set. Bake medium circles 12 to 15 minutes or until set. Cool on cookie sheets 5 minutes. Remove to wire racks; cool completely.

6. Spread medium circles with frosting; spread thin layer of frosting on backs and adhere to large circles for mouth. Add food coloring, a few drops at a time, to remaining frosting; stir until evenly colored. Spread small circles with black frosting for ears. Dot cut side of jelly beans with frosting and adhere for eyes and nose. Pipe mouth using black frosting. Let stand 10 minutes or until set.

Makes 1 dozen cookies

Chocolate Chip S'More Bites

1 package (about 16 ounces) refrigerated chocolate chip cookie dough

¾ cup semisweet chocolate chips

¼ cup plus 2 tablespoons whipping cream

½ cup marshmallow creme

½ cup sour cream

1. Preheat oven to 325°F. Spray 13×9-inch baking pan with nonstick cooking spray.

2. Press cookie dough into prepared pan, using damp hands to spread dough into even layer and cover bottom of pan. (Dough will be very thin.) Bake 20 minutes or until light golden brown and just set. Cool in pan on wire rack.

3. Meanwhile, place chocolate chips in medium bowl. Microwave cream in small bowl on HIGH 1 minute or just until simmering; pour over chocolate chips. Let stand 2 minutes; stir until smooth. Let stand 10 minutes or until mixture thickens.

4. Combine marshmallow creme and sour cream in small bowl until smooth.

5. Cut bars into 1¼-inch squares with sharp knife. For each s'more, spread scant teaspoon chocolate mixture on bottom of one square; spread scant teaspoon marshmallow mixture on bottom of second square. Press together to form s'mores.

Makes about 4 dozen s'mores

PB & J
Sandwich Cookies

Easy All-Purpose Cookie Dough (page 60)

⅓ cup plus 2 tablespoons creamy peanut butter, divided

2 tablespoons strawberry jam

3 to 4 drops red food coloring

2 tablespoons butter, softened

1 cup powdered sugar

3 tablespoons milk or half-and-half

1. Prepare dough. Divide dough in half; add 2 tablespoons peanut butter to one half and beat until blended. Add jam and food coloring to other half of dough; beat until blended. Shape dough into 10-inch logs. Wrap separately in plastic wrap; refrigerate 1 hour or until firm.

2. Preheat oven to 300°F. Cut each log into ⅓-inch-thick slices; place on ungreased cookie sheets. Bake 15 to 18 minutes or until cookies are set and lightly browned. Cool on cookie sheets 5 minutes. Remove to wire racks; cool completely.

3. For filling, beat remaining ⅓ cup peanut butter and 2 tablespoons butter in large bowl with electric mixer at medium speed until smooth. Gradually add 1 cup powdered sugar; blend well. Add milk; beat until light and fluffy. Spread about 1½ teaspoons filling over flat sides of peanut butter cookies; top with strawberry cookies.

Makes about 2½ dozen cookies

Lady Bugs

2 cups all-purpose flour
1/3 cup cornmeal
1 teaspoon baking powder
1/2 teaspoon salt
3/4 cup shortening
1/2 cup sugar

1/4 cup honey
1 egg
1/2 teaspoon vanilla
Red and black icings
Mini yellow candy-coated
chocolate pieces

1. Combine flour, cornmeal, baking powder and salt in medium bowl.

2. Beat shortening, sugar and honey in large bowl with electric mixer at medium speed until light and fluffy. Add egg and vanilla; beat until well blended. Add flour mixture at low speed until blended. Shape dough into disc. Wrap in plastic wrap; refrigerate 2 hours or overnight.

3. Preheat oven to 375°F. Divide dough into 24 equal pieces. Shape each piece into 2×1¼-inch oval; place 2 inches apart on ungreased cookie sheets.

4. Bake 10 to 12 minutes or until lightly browned. Cool on cookie sheets 2 minutes. Remove to wire racks; cool completely.

5. Decorate cookies with red and black icings and candy-coated pieces to resemble lady bugs.

Makes 2 dozen cookies

Over Easy Cookies

1 package (about 16 ounces) refrigerated break-apart sugar cookie dough (24 count)

1 package (14 ounces) white chocolate candy discs

1 cup prepared white or vanilla frosting

Yellow gel food coloring

1. Let dough stand at room temperature 5 minutes. Line cookie sheets with parchment paper.

2. Preheat oven to 325°F. Roll out dough between sheets of parchment paper to $\frac{1}{4}$-inch thickness. Cut out egg white shapes with sharp knife (approximately $3\frac{1}{2} \times 2\frac{1}{2}$-inch shapes); place 2 inches apart on prepared cookie sheets. Cut out yolks with $1\frac{1}{4}$-inch round cookie cutter. Place egg yolks 1 inch apart on separate prepared cookie sheet. Refrigerate 15 minutes.

3. Bake egg whites 15 to 17 minutes or until set. Bake egg yolks 10 to 12 minutes or until set. Cool on cookie sheets 5 minutes. Remove to wire racks; cool completely.

4. Microwave candy discs in medium microwavable bowl on HIGH 1 minute. Stir. Microwave at additional 15-second intervals until smooth and spreadable. Spread over egg whites. Let stand on wire racks 10 minutes or until set.

5. Tint frosting with food coloring until desired shade of yellow is reached. Spread over egg yolks. Spread thin layer of frosting on back of egg yolks and adhere to egg whites. Let stand 10 minutes or until set.

Makes about 1 dozen cookies

Makin' Bacon Cookies

1 package (about 16 ounces) refrigerated break-apart sugar cookie dough (24 count)

½ cup water, divided
Red, brown and yellow gel food colorings

1. Let dough stand at room temperature 5 minutes. Line cookie sheets with parchment paper.

2. Preheat oven to 325°F. Roll out dough between sheets of parchment paper to ¼-inch thickness. Cut out bacon shapes with sharp knife (approximately 3½×1-inch shapes). Place 2 inches apart on prepared cookie sheets. Refrigerate 15 minutes.

3. Bake 13 to 15 minutes or until set. Cool on cookie sheets 5 minutes. Remove to wire racks; cool completely.

4. Place ¼ cup water in small bowl. Tint with red and brown food coloring until desired shade of brown is reached. Place remaining ¼ cup water in another small bowl. Tint with red and yellow food coloring until desired shade of orange is reached. Paint cookies to resemble bacon with small clean paintbrushes,* using as little water as possible for color to saturate. Leave some areas unpainted to resemble bacon fat. Let stand 1 hour or until dry.

*Do not use paintbrushes that have been used for anything other than food.

Makes about 2 dozen cookies

Swashbuckling Pirates

3½ cups all-purpose flour

1 teaspoon salt

1½ cups sugar

1 cup (2 sticks) butter, softened

2 eggs

2 teaspoons vanilla

Royal Icing (recipe follows)

Pink, orange, yellow and red gel food colorings

Red string licorice

Red candy-coated chocolate pieces

Black decorating gel

Mini semisweet chocolate chips

1. Combine flour and salt in medium bowl.

2. Beat sugar and butter in large bowl with electric mixer at medium speed until light and fluffy. Add eggs, one at a time, beating until blended after each addition. Add vanilla; beat until blended. Gradually add flour mixture at low speed until well blended. Shape dough into two discs. Wrap separately in plastic wrap; refrigerate 1 hour or until firm.

3. Preheat oven to 350°F. Line cookie sheets with parchment paper. Roll out dough on lightly floured surface to ¼-inch thickness. Cut out circles with 3¼-inch round cookie cutter. Place 1 inch apart on prepared cookie sheets. Refrigerate 15 minutes.

4. Bake 15 to 17 minutes or until set. Cool on cookie sheets 5 minutes. Remove to wire racks; cool completely.

5. Prepare Royal Icing. Reserve one third of icing in small bowl. Tint remaining icing with pink, orange and yellow food colorings until desired shade of peach is reached. Spread two thirds of each cookie with peach icing. Let stand 10 minutes or until set.

6. Spread remaining one third of each cookie with reserved white icing. Cut licorice for edge of bandana and mouth; press into icing. Press chocolate pieces into white icing. Let stand 10 minutes or until set.

7. Pipe eye patch using decorating gel. Pipe eye with white icing; press mini chocolate chip into center of eye. Press mini chocolate chips into icing for mustache. Let stand 10 minutes or until set.

Makes about 1½ dozen cookies

ROYAL ICING: Combine 4 cups powdered sugar, 6 tablespoons water and 3 tablespoons meringue powder in medium bowl. Beat with electric mixer at high speed 7 to 10 minutes or until soft peaks form. Cover surface with plastic wrap until needed. Makes about 2 cups.

Happy Face Oatmeal Monsters

1½ cups all-purpose flour

1 teaspoon baking soda

½ teaspoon salt

1 cup (2 sticks) butter, softened

1 cup packed brown sugar

2 eggs

1 teaspoon vanilla

2 cups quick oats

Granulated sugar

28 candy-coated chocolate pieces

Red string licorice

1. Preheat oven to 350°F. Combine flour, baking soda and salt in small bowl.

2. Beat butter and brown sugar in large bowl with electric mixer at medium speed until light and fluffy. Beat in eggs, one at a time, until well blended. Beat in vanilla. Gradually beat in flour mixture at low speed until blended. Stir in oats.

3. Drop dough by level ¼-cupfuls 3 inches apart onto ungreased cookie sheets. Flatten dough with bottom of glass that has been dipped in granulated sugar until dough is 2 inches in diameter. Press chocolate pieces into cookies for eyes; use licorice for mouth.

4. Bake 12 to 14 minutes or until cookies are set and edges are golden brown. Cool on cookie sheets 2 minutes. Remove to wire racks; cool completely.

Makes about 14 cookies

Cookie Pop Bouquets

1 package (about 15 ounces) yellow cake mix
½ cup all-purpose flour
½ cup (1 stick) butter, melted
2 eggs, lightly beaten
2 tablespoons honey

1 container (16 ounces) white frosting
Colored sugar, assorted sprinkles and decors

1. Combine cake mix, flour, butter, eggs and honey in large bowl until well blended. Cover and refrigerate 30 minutes.

2. Preheat oven to 375°F. Line cookie sheets with parchment paper.

3. Roll out dough to ½-inch thickness on floured surface. Cut out shapes with assorted cookie cutters; place 2 inches apart on prepared cookie sheets. Place lollipop stick under and halfway up each cookie; press lightly.

4. Bake 10 to 12 minutes or until edges are lightly browned. Cool on cookie sheets 3 minutes. Remove to wire racks; cool completely.

5. Frost cookies; decorate as desired.

Makes about 2 dozen cookie pops

Metric Conversion Chart

VOLUME MEASUREMENTS (dry)

¹/₈ teaspoon = 0.5 mL
¹/₄ teaspoon = 1 mL
¹/₂ teaspoon = 2 mL
³/₄ teaspoon = 4 mL
1 teaspoon = 5 mL
1 tablespoon = 15 mL
2 tablespoons = 30 mL
¹/₄ cup = 60 mL
¹/₃ cup = 75 mL
¹/₂ cup = 125 mL
²/₃ cup = 150 mL
³/₄ cup = 175 mL
1 cup = 250 mL
2 cups = 1 pint = 500 mL
3 cups = 750 mL
4 cups = 1 quart = 1 L

VOLUME MEASUREMENTS (fluid)

1 fluid ounce (2 tablespoons) = 30 mL
4 fluid ounces (¹/₂ cup) = 125 mL
8 fluid ounces (1 cup) = 250 mL
12 fluid ounces (1¹/₂ cups) = 375 mL
16 fluid ounces (2 cups) = 500 mL

WEIGHTS (mass)

¹/₂ ounce = 15 g
1 ounce = 30 g
3 ounces = 90 g
4 ounces = 120 g
8 ounces = 225 g
10 ounces = 285 g
12 ounces = 360 g
16 ounces = 1 pound = 450 g

DIMENSIONS

¹/₁₆ inch = 2 mm
¹/₈ inch = 3 mm
¹/₄ inch = 6 mm
¹/₂ inch = 1.5 cm
³/₄ inch = 2 cm
1 inch = 2.5 cm

OVEN TEMPERATURES

250°F = 120°C
275°F = 140°C
300°F = 150°C
325°F = 160°C
350°F = 180°C
375°F = 190°C
400°F = 200°C
425°F = 220°C
450°F = 230°C

BAKING PAN SIZES

Utensil	Size in Inches/Quarts	Metric Volume	Size in Centimeters
Baking or Cake Pan (square or rectangular)	8×8×2	2 L	20×20×5
	9×9×2	2.5 L	23×23×5
	12×8×2	3 L	30×20×5
	13×9×2	3.5 L	33×23×5
Loaf Pan	8×4×3	1.5 L	20×10×7
	9×5×3	2 L	23×13×7
Round Layer Cake Pan	8×1½	1.2 L	20×4
	9×1½	1.5 L	23×4
Pie Plate	8×1¼	750 mL	20×3
	9×1¼	1 L	23×3
Baking Dish or Casserole	1 quart	1 L	—
	1½ quart	1.5 L	—
	2 quart	2 L	—